# THIS DOESN'T MAKE ME AN EXPERT

and other lies I told myself while building a successful direct sales business.

## Sasha Sweder

Sasha Sweder

©2019 Sasha Sweder All Rights Reserved. No part of this publication may be reproduced, distributed, or transmitted in any form or by any means, including photocopying, recording, or other electronic or mechanical methods, without the prior written permission of the publisher, except in the case of brief quotations embodied in critical reviews and certain other noncommercial uses permitted by copyright law.

For permission requests, email the publisher, addressed "Attention: Permissions Coordinator," at the email address below.

Sasha Sweder
poshswederside@gmail.com
www.SashaSweder.com

Ordering Information:
Quantity sales. Special discounts are available on quantity purchases by corporations, associations, and others. For details, contact the publisher at the email address above.
Orders by U.S. trade bookstores and wholesalers.
Please contact Big Distribution: Tel: (908) 705-7165 or visit www.SashaSweder.com.

Printed in the United States of America
ISBN: 9781793325044
Imprint: Independently published
First Printing, 2019

This book is memoir and instructional. It reflects the author's present recollections of experiences over time. Some names and characteristics have been changed, some events have been compressed, and some dialogue has been recreated. The advice and strategies found within may not be suitable for every situation. This work is sold with the understanding that neither the author nor the publisher are held responsible for the results accrued from the advice in this book.

Credits
Cover Art and Photo by Sasha Sweder
Editing by Kristina Skiba, David Sweder
Beta Readers: Shannon Bissett, Tanya Miller, Elizabeth Nile, Shana Boyer, Jordan Bridge, Robyn Darby, Samantha Moore, Natalie Grey and 200 of my closest friends.

# CONTENTS

| | |
|---|---|
| Copyright | 2 |
| CHAPTER 1 NO, SHE DIDN'T. | 5 |
| Intro | |
| CHAPTER 2 NO, SHE WON'T. | 25 |
| Goals | |
| CHAPTER 3 NO, SHE CAN'T | 55 |
| Launching a business. | |
| CHAPTER 4 NO, SHE DOESN'T | 77 |
| Customer Service, Sales, & Marketing | |
| CHAPTER 5 NO, SHE SHOULDN'T | 114 |
| Branding & Marketing | |
| CHAPTER 6 NO, SHE COULDN'T. | 145 |
| Social Media | |
| CHAPTER 7 NO, SHE WASN'T | 185 |
| Parties and Vendor events | |
| CHAPTER 8 NO, SHE iSN'T | 210 |
| Leadership and Relationships | |
| CHAPTER 9 I can, I will, I just did. | 221 |
| Lessons I have learned | |
| MASTER BOOK LIST FOR LEARNING STUFF AND ALSO THINGS | 240 |
| Epilogue | 253 |
| Acknowledgements | 256 |

*Dedicated to my kids. You can do scary things. I'll be cheering.*

## CHAPTER 1
# NO, SHE DIDN'T.
### No, she didn't join that company.

No one tells you about how the people around you will react to your decision to start a direct sales company after ordering your first starter kit. I often jokingly compare it to the first few moments after telling people close to you that you are getting married or having a baby.

It all starts with a hushed, room announcement where everyone is watching or maybe a social media status that feels just as anxiety filled. Followed by, the reaction of hesitant smiles and "congrats" that friends share because they have listened to 30 seconds of what you said but are confident that whatever you are saying is a HAPPY statement. So in pure peer pressure fashion, they just copy the response of the person that comments first or they have looked around the room to mimic the responses of the people sitting in front of them. Then, comes the "well-intentioned" Q&A session where people try to pinpoint the flaws in your plan in a public forum. "So have you picked a date for the wedding?" which is actually a nicely phrased "pick the month I did or you are wrong because December is reserved for marriages that last. I am not biased, I just happened to be married in December." Or the, "So excited you are having a baby! Are you going to bottle feed?" Which is equivalent to "Bottle is best, cups are for quitters, and I know this because I have a dog that I read graphic novels to." In this case, the question asked will be "So excited you are starting a business, but isn't that one of those pyramid schemes?" The question cuts like a knife, right to the point and tends to come from a family member or friend packed with well-intended concern. Unfortunately, so many are misinformed about direct sales that they can't just give you five minutes to sit and be excited, scared, or whatever you happen to be feeling. This question comes from decades of stories of friends and family members falling for "get rich quick" schemes or cabinets full of Tupperware and SkinSoSoft then seeing newscasts or documentaries about the scary after effects of companies that broke the law, were dishonest, and sold consultants a ton of lies. Many businesses die before they even start because of this scary question. This question is as loaded as asking about medication during labor and during breastfeeding or asking about whether you are getting married in a house of worship or a restaurant, which are topics that have been featured on the news and can cause a family meal to erupt into fights. This is the first off-ramp for your "big life choice", so if you got past this great job!

Finally, the awkward silence of loved ones after your life has changed and they have decided how they feel about it. You have been engaged for a few months, you are beginning to show in your pregnancy, or are now the proud owner of a business. They have decided to support you or not. This is actually the moment when you have to make a choice, do you let anxiety kick in and question everything you have done to this point or do you get down to business and make good on your highly anticipated public announcement? For a wedding, it is time to pick that date, venue, and dress! For a baby, it is time to schedule those doctor visits and change your lifestyle. For a business, it is time to schedule that launch party and grow your client list! All three have the potential to be fun and emotionally enriching when surrounded by people you love. However, the moment it is just you in a room with a computer planning the necessary steps to get your business off the ground, you may be met with the same crippling fears that caused some of the strongest people I know to crumble or quit. Fears of judgment from family and friends fears from society telling you that you made a poor choice, fears about finances, or just fears of inadequacy when you keep hearing NO from your strongest support system. The thing to keep in mind is, this is not abnormal for any business opportunity. Be careful, this is the second off-ramp so let's dig in.

The first issue for debate that comes up is people questioning the validity of your business before you even open(or marriage or parenting ability if you are following along). I have seen people refuse my info the second I brought up a starter kit because I will never be a real business woman unless I have a storefront. While I can debate that this is actually an attack on an industry that is predominately women trying to make ends met, let's go a different way and focus on "direct sales vs a storefront" because it is really helping people have access to a sales career in a more cost-effective way if done right. This judgment ignores the affordable convenience of direct sales starter kits compared to opening a storefront or franchise. A storefront or franchise business requires legal documentation to register your business, utilities for electricity/water/garbage/sewage/gas, a location you own or rent, advertising, logos and branding, personnel training, bookkeeping, and product inventory of the goods you wish to sell. (I feel like I am missing a ton in that list.) Direct Sales companies, on the other hand, alleviate the costs of the aforementioned requirements to start a business in sales. At the corporate level, they provide the necessary training to work a business successfully, pay you commissions on sales, manage product inventory and shipping, and handle all of the other costly overhead associated with running a storefront or franchise. Depending on the company you join and the team you build; you can use the box of stuff for yourself, you can start a hobby business where you dip your toe in the water, or you can hold your nose and run for the deep end as I did. The hard part of this fight comes with accountability and commitment to actually build or just treating the opportunity as a hobby. Direct Sales hobbyists rarely calculate ROI(Return on Investment) or budget for advertising outside of their warm markets. This can mimic the results of a person opening a pizza place from your kitchen and expecting the only family to buy pizza for all three meals for decades. Unrealistic and dangerous financial decisions will ensue either way! So when comparing the two options, it is important to be treating both opportunities equally because both can turn disastrous when all circumstances are accounted for. So it is not just direct sales, has anyone asked all the cupcake bakeries that opened in the 2000s how great life is after a trend changes? I can tell you from personal experience it can be difficult either way. But again, you either know this or refused to understand this perspective.

The second issue I ran into is people love to tell me "No". Over the years I have learned that it is more about them than me, but nevertheless, I hear it way more than most so I have gotten used to it. When my anxiety is really bad I can even catch myself telling me "no" before others have a chance because I have heard the word so much that it is instincts for me to see limits. People will say I can't do something based on their own fears of failure or they will tell me "No" because of their own experiences with whatever I am about to try. People have told me "No" because I am a loud and super Italian Jersey Girl in the South or "No" because I am the anxiety-driven awkward duck instead of the eloquently worded picture perfect example. They have told me "No" because of my name sounding unique and not simple and told me "No" because they decided I wasn't like them before I sat down at the table. They have told me "No" because I lacked resources, education, or time to fully explain my big ideas. They have told me "No" because I have kids or because of how often I have relocated. They said "No" when I looked too young and "No" when they think I look older than a millennial. They have said "No" to me but "Yes" to others because they could say my words and ideas in a more coherent fashion. They have told me "No" because of my gender, lack of religion, family status, and race. I'm sure this is all starting to sound very familiar, if not, relatable. While I am confident that I am BY FAR not the most limited person in this world, I have grown a coping mechanism to get by not always asking or by ignoring responses. (I am confident it is at this point my father is having flashbacks of my teenage years while reading this. Hi Dad!) Through all of the "No" in my life the only time it really stopped me from achieving, was when I let it block me from seeing a path forward and that happened way more often than I would like to admit. The effort to always fight back against it or becoming defensive wasted my energy. I stopped myself short of my goals on so many occasions because I believed that other people had the right to tell me where to go, how to sit, what I could do, and when I could do it. Many times I could have corrected people that thought that I was actually lazy, stubborn, or selfish but I also learned that was pointless. Come to realize over the years, that many of my shortcomings in life and in business were my fault because I did not understand that "No" just means not right now or not in this manner.

So the same problem happened when I dreamed of bright pink and bold business choices. People kept telling me it wouldn't work out and at first, I believed them because it was a habit to believe others before listening to my own intuition. To be honest with myself, I am not even confident I really knew what "working out" would look like in the end without seeing the success stories of people that traveled before me. I had to learn that roadblocks required more creativity and innovation. Anyone can tell me no, it is my job to figure out how to get it done anyway. Especially if I believe that what I am fighting for is important and connects with my overall vision for how I want my life. As my business grew, I learned it was much closer to a "real" business opportunity than I had ever been told, but I had to be careful and strategic. My bills were getting paid for once! The sales numbers started to line up and people started to share the products just like a bakery or restaurant because they were good. The product began to be recognized in my circles just as much as any store-bought product. I learned how to not spam and noticed patterns where everyone was following crowds. I learned quickly I didn't need everyone to buy from me, as long as I had people that loved the products and appreciated my personal touch they remained loyal. This reinforced my gut instinct to put quality customer service strategies ahead of focusing on tactics that pushed me to need lots of people to buy my products once. After a short period of time, people could say whatever the heck they wanted and it was irrelevant because I had numbers to prove that opinions about my business were not going to stop me. It became a battle of opinions versus facts, and the facts were winning. The biggest keys to this much progress we will be discussed in coming chapters, but the foundation of this growth came from learning something new every day. Oddly enough, just like getting married and having your first baby.

Direct Sales can change your life if you manage it all like a real business or it can cost you a ton, beat you down, and put you in debt that only emotional choices can create. It is often ignored how much of this is a mental game. It required learning to stay in my own lane, which is hard when it is easy to get competitive. Comfort zones and self-imposed excuses became my real obstacles. I HATE excel spreadsheets and have had to learn so much more than I ever wanted to. I have made expensive mistakes and had to find a way to rally with $5 in my bank account to finish out the month strong despite those mistakes. I have had to stand up tall in rooms that didn't see me as deserving to be in them and learned you have to take yourself seriously way before those around you will consider your business, a real business. Yes, you may not always be seen as legit, but adult entertainers don't quit work purely because others don't believe in their work. Maybe not the best example but yeah.

You have to invest in you, be proud of you, be excited about you, and motivate you. You have to push yourself when it isn't easy because it won't always be bath bombs and magic. You have to recognize how far you have come, show no fear when you look crazy throwing confetti on yourself to celebrate your achievements. You also have to stay humble but productive. In this industry, no one tells you, that you control your destiny. It is one of the scariest, most beautiful, and challenging endeavors you will ever embark upon.

In the next chapters, I hope to help you remember that you are truly the person not just in control of your business, but also your life. You have the power inside you to do great things even if the whole world tries to tell you otherwise. I gave up my power when I was growing up because I believed those around me knew better than I did. It took a crazy polka dot box of soap to teach me that I can have everything I want, even if others don't understand my industry, even if the odds are against me, and even if I am not perfect at everything I do. Yes, I have time to take care of me. Yes, I do get to decide how I make money. Yes, I can set my hours around my kid's schooling. Yes, I can change the financial future of my family. Yes, I can look fear in the face and beat down my depression. Yes, I can break crippling mental health issues. Yes, I can build a family of women without constantly comparing ourselves. Yes, I can lead a team I build and not wait for someone to decide I am ready. Yes, I can teach other people to also change their lives. Direct Sales is part of my journey so I will be sharing the lessons I learned, but so is my time in the kitchen, parenting, life as a military spouse, and my marriage. Make no mistake, this book is packed with life lessons on how to buck the trends because that is what I have been able to do when I grabbed that power back. I have had to fight hard for the person I am now, I can't wait to help you do that also. Let's go!

CHAPTER 2

## NO, SHE WON'T.
No, she won't hit her goals.

..................................................

Goal setting is not something that comes naturally to me. I am confident people have tried to teach me how to set goals in many avenues of my life and I ignored every person until recently. Ignored is a harsh word for it, "avoided learning or listening" is probably more accurate. I often have no idea where to even start and then I give up if I hit obstacles. (Remember all the people telling me no?) In school, I could not connect how grades at the end of the marking period connected with the homework I refused to do because I had no idea what the significance of homework was. Now that I have kids, I see that it is for practice. My father once tried to bribe me into getting good grades by offering to pay for each grade letter above a B, ignoring the fact that I had no idea HOW to get a grade above a B(hint: I bet the homework would have told me how).

I also have an issue with focus, which in itself manifests some of the most annoying habits that prevent me from completing basic tasks, let alone meeting my goals. For example, I have a tendency to leave cabinet doors or drawers open because I forgot I was even there. I also require all of the ingredients needed to finish a project before starting, then forget what I was working on once distracted. I will start a project in the middle of the dining table and never finish. All of these habits culminate into a snowball of incomplete tasks. For years, I would take the time necessary to set a financial budget only to completely ignore it whenever it became time to spend money. I would refuse to ask for the help of any kind and when I received help, lacked the discipline to follow through. I would make excuses as to why I won't or can't do it. I would ignore and avoid decisions all together if I felt like I couldn't control the outcome. I have the attention span of a gnat, at times. I know this about myself and own all of it! A waning attention span can drive people around me to occasional murderous rage but it is something I have learned to accept about myself. Luckily, I am able to balance the effects of my shortcomings with being super fun. I am kidding, kind of.

The first step to changing these habits is acknowledging you have a problem. Goal setting can be a PROBLEM. I make jokes but this doesn't mean I love this about myself, I have found it can be one of those traits that hinder my progress over and over again. It can cost me time, money, and friendships. Have you ever forgotten to ship things or lost a parking ticket? I categorize daily or important tasks into goal setting because setting a goal means you commit to doing something to completion. The entire idea of having to commit to something causes my anxiety to rise. What if I forget? What if I let someone down? What if I don't finish on time? The difficulty in knowing about your weaknesses is the fear of repeating your mistakes. Questions rush into my brain and instead of solving these VALID questions, having noticed them on my worst days, the only solution I come to is RUNNING FAR AWAY! Most often towards a book or tv show worth binge watching.

There are only two times in my life where this seems to not be the case: my marriage and my business, two relationships that I have unyielding commitment despite everything else in my world constantly changing. I sat down a few months ago to really think about why this is.

*David & Sasha*

Meet my handsome and crazy high school sweetheart. After almost 6 years of high school and college together, we married in 2005. He has taught me so much about balancing a spontaneous life and responsibility. He is my rock when my life is unstable. He had the discipline to go from JROTC in high school to ROTC at The Citadel to 9 years in the Air Force. He started a bank account in high school, held the same job for more than 2 years in college. He started a retirement fund, a college fund for our unborn children, and covered us for insurance. After graduating college, he also paid almost all of our bills with his Air Force paycheck. He has his own faults, but realistically, our relationship has centered around one being spontaneous and the other being consistent. Can you guess which I am? During the same period of time from '00-'04, I moved 6 times, enrolled in 3 schools, held over 10 jobs, definitely went through a ton of clothes, and barely paid my bills on time. Did I mention I am fun? I made him move to Florida for my employment with Disney, add Disney magic to the house during holidays, dragged him on to dance floors, brought home new animal friends, and reminded him to take life less serious! He is the side of the house that pays the bills after budgeting on a spreadsheet, I am the side of the house that throws glitter and buys a llama with her savings. Everyone needs a person like that in their life, they remind you to live. He is my Greg, I am his Dharma. Wait let's update that a bit. He is my Ben, I am his Leslie.

I can almost guarantee his balance, stability, and support helped me keep going when I was young and during our marriage. He was the one to tell me to get an oil change on my first car after helping to teach me how to drive. He was the reason I moved outside of New Jersey as an 18-year-old after 9/11 and the reason I never needed to move back home. When I started crying in a hotel room because I had packed up my life into a Ford Escort, he knew I would be fine and we could figure it all out no matter what. He was also the person that helped me have things I never thought I would have like Life Insurance, a consistent roof over my head, and a Retirement fund. Life has not been easy so I can see how this could be seen as putting all the pressure on him which I am conscious of. As I grew up, I learned this is without a doubt a coping mechanism. I am emotional, he is rational. He is focused, strategic, and can be stronger than me when facing problems. I lean on him, just as he leans on me. David has taught me that all the oars need to be in the water to get anywhere as a team. And yes, even with all the stuff he covers he leans on me also. Teamwork.

Parenthood was our next challenge as a couple in 2007. I stayed home from 2007-2013, I am not the perfect mom but I love my babies with all the care and well-intended guilt trips a Jewish Italian can muster. He is a modern father, which in our house means he cooks and cleans as much as I do. We divide household tasks based on who is traveling and home. We vaccinated both our children, we were such rebels at the time. I breastfed both kids for 2 years and when we lost the third baby we all moved on to battle potty training, poorly, as a family. We both got up in the middle of the night, shared feeding solid foods, and changed diapers. My kids are now 9 & 11 and they get to make messes because we encourage creativity. I love trips to the movies, being considered an adult on field trips, and "never yelling" when my daughter paints her furniture and toys. (I think this generation calls it "DIY crafts".) I pick my battles and prioritize even if it doesn't seem like it. I try to be reasonable with myself so not every dish gets clean by bedtime but every kid is bathed. Laundry and I are in a life long battle to see who will outlast the other. I also look forward to every day we get a babysitter. That being said, I love that I have gotten to be there for almost every bedtime kiss. I have also seen almost every assembly, helped with all the fundraisers, pushed them to get to after-school activities, and hopefully, they see that life

## This Doesn't Make Me An Expert

doesn't have to be perfect to be great. I consider that to be a blessing 11 years into parenthood.

For me, setting goals and getting things done in a house with kids can be like throwing spaghetti against a wall hoping it will stick, you are either going to stand around yelling while the kids watch you lose your mind OR you are going to calmly accept progress over perfection. I save all my energy for the big fights like IEP meetings, teacher conferences, and doctor appointments. Our oldest was diagnosed with ADHD, Dysgraphia, and Social Anxiety in 2017. Teamwork is an understatement when you are sitting in an expulsion hearing because the school is refusing to provide your son services. Goals change when you start to assemble a group of professionals to help teach your son the social skills he has been missing. Everyone learns how to be realistic and thankful for the obstacles we start tackling. Have I said the word "reasonable" enough to paint a picture? We aren't even trying for perfection at this point, our goal is set to "productive and progressing." I can celebrate that they got to school on time and no referrals to the Principal or I can get angry about the fact that they need to buy lunch, left completed homework on the counter at home, and might have a cowlick in their hair. I'd rather celebrate every success. Parenting in my house has taught me that it doesn't matter what anyone else on the outside sees as long as the people on the team are healthy and happy. Teamwork, literally, makes our dream work. Our biggest goal is to suck less tomorrow, always progressing towards growth.

*Sasha & Direct Sales*

The second time in my life was with my direct sales business. I had all the same odds against me succeeding as I did marrying my high school sweetheart but I still jumped in. I had no clue how I was going to do this but I started with what I could control. I just started with what products I loved to use! When I was considering to join, I had placed one large order with my company and loved the bath stuff I had received. I also really loved the shea butter sticks packed with essential oils that I could finally afford. To prepare for Dave returning from his deployment, I went for a facial with an expensive company and came home with a list of items almost identical to the starter kit that totaled over $250. I purchased my starter kit at 11:35 pm on November 19, 2013, for $99 plus tax and shipping. The giant box showed up on my doorstep the day after we picked Dave up from the airport. I opened up the pamphlet of info in the kit and I set my eyes on selling $200 with no successful experience selling skincare. Next, I set up a Facebook event with 25 friends and sent out 25 bags of samples. My family got in the car and drove to Disney on R & R with Dave after he arrived home from his deployment. Most of the items I sent out spilled or failed to arrive. Nervously, I shared info in the event about products I had purchased and had people share which products they loved out of the items that arrived intact. This had to work, I had no money to buy anything and really hated the idea of getting a job when I got back. We needed money to pay down debt and I was already told that not a single family dollar was getting invested in my business.

The first order on my website came from a friend when we arrived at a hotel in Missouri, halfway to Disney. She placed an order with her mother! I was halfway to the first goal of $200 and something started to seem different about this company. People were actually buying! This gave me such a push of confidence that I got up the nerve to post in the event that I was halfway to my first goal! Soon after, more orders came in and I hit my first goal with my company. I closed up the party and had earned the 15-day quick start reward points to cover more business supplies on top of the product credits! I realized I could give my customers the product credits as a thank you as long as I could earn my quick start business rewards. Then I wouldn't need to spend more money and I could make a complete profit off the sales!

It was time to focus on the next goal: $500 total in the first 30 days and 1 new teammate. This would help me earn about $60 in business supplies covered! This time I had a plan on how to get the sales confidently, there was one big issue, I needed a teammate. Where was I going to get one of those? Adding a teammate was one of the first real fears I had about this business after the pyramid scheme conversations. I decided that because this appeared to be difficult, I should focus on that first! How the heck was I going to 'recruit' someone to join my team?! At the time, I could confidently say that I could lead a team, but who would be willing to spend $99 and join me?! Who would trust me that much?! As people started to order, I made sure I thanked them in the facebook event! Little did I know that I was showing people that my business was growing in credibility and trust. I had a few friends start to ask questions about the starter kit and I was a bit unprepared. I would tell them I didn't know but would always get back to them. I had looked at the info but didn't have it with me while I was on the road.

On December 1st, my company launched the first version of an amazing training program and my world went crazy! Most of my circle had never participated in Direct Sales so we were all worried that we didn't know how to run a business. The training we received made recruiting a little easier and made people feel more confident that they could learn how. People were coming out of the woodwork fast and many I had not even considered asking because I never thought they would be looking for the opportunity! The first person to join my team was a school teacher, "Tara" (Name changed to protect the awesome). I can still picture the staircase I was staring at praying she would say yes the first time I asked her to join my team, AND SHE DID! She applied her teaching skills to help grow her team and ended up becoming a leader in a little over 2 years. But in those first few moments, I had no clue she was looking for a company to try until she came to me! I learned very quickly that I had to consider everyone a potential teammate, I needed to ask everyone. She had more experience from direct sales parties than I did so I was able to learn from her and she had also built connections while in North Dakota from leading one of the military spouse groups. I had already seen her leadership skills in action, so I was ecstatic to have her be the first to join my team. Tara helped me hit the scary part of my goal for my first month, ONE new teammate. Now I had to focus on sales again.

Whoops! I did it again! I was refocusing on sales and handing out samples to every person I talked to from Florida to Colorado on our road trip. On the way back home in a grocery store in Missouri, I met "May". She seemed frustrated about finances when I met her. I had only enough cash on me to buy a cup of mashed potatoes and yet, she listened to me talk all about my company after I gave her a bundle of samples to pamper herself after a hard day at work at the Deli counter. After she joined our team, I started to focus the entire team on hitting $1000 total in personal sales and ranking up to the first level because it would get us all 5% raises. I went to the mall and picked out earrings as the first thing I would give to my team when we all hit the rank advancement. I sent May a pair and she gave them to her daughter after she earned them for hitting $1000 in sales. We all cried happy tears as a team when she posted that her daughter was so emotional about getting her first sparkle earrings ever, May taught me that my business could make a big deal to my customers but could also bless the lives of my teammates. This lesson helped me shape my leadership style for the next 5 years. In the first moments as a team, I learned that pushing to sales goals together can be empowering for everyone! The trick was to not focus on the rank advancement that would only help me but to work together so we all could celebrate. Pushing myself to hit sales goals helped me get more rewards but seeing us all earn the rewards encouraged us all to feel like superheroes. Teamwork.

At that point I started to feel like I had a rhythm for the team, focus on a team goal and crush it together. Once again, I conquered a scary goal and grew stronger, this time with others to hold me accountable. I would set a goal to add one more friend to the team or hit $500-1000 and we all pushed. If someone fell behind, we would call and brainstorm ideas.

Our leaders never pressured us, they knew what we all really needed was ideas on HOW to crush goals. As the leader, I would make sure we all did a training video on the team page when someone had a breakthrough or shared resources. We all worked together, and our families started to see the successes in our financial gains. If a new teammate hit $200 that was $50 more dollars in the family bank account. If they sold $500, that was $125 for groceries. We posted every success. Goals started to become fun to set and were continually rewarding to crush. There was always a reward! I would set up a party every week and sell $250 and start over again the next week, this was a steady paycheck I was able to earn from my couch after the kids went to bed. This was the dream to the people around me, stay at home parents that couldn't get a job that paid enough to pay daycare and the bills.

The first 90 days of my business I learned so much about myself but the biggest lessons came from those around me. Goal setting can be fun even if you are terrified to do what you are committing to do. I learned that the first obstacles are either going to make you stronger and more determined or undermine you. You decide how you react. I could have given up on a business that went on to sell over $11 million dollars in the product because the first samples I sent out spilled or got lost in the mail. Instead, I got creative. I learned that teammates can come from anywhere, people are always watching how you are doing at first so show enthusiasm, not fear. If you are telling people that you are doing great, some will judge but more will be curious. Focus effort on those that are curious and teach them how to do everything you are doing to succeed. I also learned that the gifts and incentives can be a big deal to the people earning them, so be strategic when picking them out and make sure that you are helping as many of your team members within reasonable financial expectations. The entire team wins when working towards a big scary goal together, even if you as the leader are scared to push. If they team bonds over the fears, they can move a mountain because of the mutual support in a safe space. Create that safe space and then help them build strong bonds.

*#Goals*

My two biggest examples of success when it

## This Doesn't Make Me An Expert

comes to goal setting had many similarities, as I am sure you can find in moments you rocked goal setting also. Give yourself grace! Both examples gave me a ton of reinforcement to keep going even if I wasn't doing everything perfectly. Both have given me small opportunities to build up the strength to tackle the next challenge. When I would forget to stay focused and accountable, honest communication would put me back on track without making it a catastrophe. Feedback pushed me forward, support to keep going from my team would get me even farther. There is always a chance to get back up and try to do better. Same with my business, small goals lead up to bigger goals when I was more experienced and stronger. Both have given me room to have fun and experience life with magic and messes, but both brought me back down to earth when I needed it. I was able to create a vision for our team future in the first 90 days as a team that would work together. That was probably the best goal I could have set.

*Let's start with real goals and
a vision board.*

We are going to start with a real-life goal setting. Not those fluffy or over-intellectual version, but the one that's going to actually drive you. There is not a single person that is exactly the same as the next so why should we treat your goals as anything different. No dream board/goal board/vision board should be either.

A wise person once did a presentation for a group of people and asked a person in the front row what their goal was, they said to pay off debt. Great! If that causes you passion, awesome. Instead, he looked in her eyes and could see that was her canned answer so he pushed her. "What's your real goal? The one you think about and dream about and hunger for?" Without a second thought, it poured out of her: "Shoes!" Stop setting the goals that everyone else needs from you, or you feel you have to, set a goal you actually care about from your toes to your nose to be successful!

*Vision Board Challenge*

1. **Answer these questions:**
   -Who do you need in your circle to get to the next level and learn from?
   -What does a 'better life' look like visually?

-What are your biggest priorities in each area of your life? Family, Career, Financially, and physically?

-Are there material items that have price tags? Print out pictures.

-Are there promotions and goals you need to reach for to gain access to the info or rewards to get to the next step? Print out the info.

-Why are these items and goals important to you and how do they connect with the vision for a better life that you are creating?

2.**Get crafty and print out or cut out images to match your answers.** Either put these images in your workspace on a board or in a place you see every day like your phone background. This board will be complete when you can stand back and you start to see a path create itself. I order you to surf the Internet and shop like you are creating a life today.

3. **If you have ever been jealous of something someone did, something your leader can do, somewhere a friend went on a trip to, maybe the woman down the street that works for 4 hours a day...**you need pictures, prices, locations so in-depth you can smell the food, you need to see the numbers, a visual to see the actions like a 5k with a workout. This can go on your wall for the family to see, in a new notebook, on your mirror, or on your lock screen. You need it to be somewhere you see it daily or weekly. You need big goals like Paris and small goals like Starbucks. Buy the shoes! You will know when you are done when you can feel the life you want in front of you in magazine clip-

pings or google images or whatever. When you are done post a picture on social and tag me so we can all support you and your real goals.

## CHAPTER 3
## NO, SHE CAN'T.
No, she can't launch a legit business from home.

..................................................

I have not checked your resume but I am assuming you have not built a building with your bare hands before, neither have I honestly but the best analogies I could think of either involved planning a party or building a building...If I went with planning a party, you may get confused so let's take a journey together and act like I have built a house. I want to remind you that I am speaking in basic terms because I fear you will think I have any experience in this and I do not. It is an analogy.

I want to introduce you to the 5 Ps. Most like

the 3 P's(Product, Process, People) or the 4 P's( Price, Promotion, Placement, Product), but we are going to blend these and build a store.

*Why do you sell it? Personal*

If you are going to build a strong business you need to know who your business is serving(customers or guests) and who is serving them(employees or teammates)! While many feel that a person should start by seeing a need and solving that need with a product, I would actually suggest seeing a need and solving it with a service. A great product can solve a need but can become one dimensional if you don't understand how to then scale your company to include more items. If you do not understand the person that is buying your first product will inspire you to build to the next. So it all really starts with serving that person's needs.

If you are considering joining a Direct Sales business that means, understand the purchasing needs of the people around you. Are they needing a certain service like the ability to destress? What products would support that need? Maybe they need a way to save on groceries or pay the bills without paying for daycare also? How can you help them? Know your people and help them.

If we imagine these are the walls, your reason for doing this is the framework for everything else. So in this analogy, my walls are a store that will serve people the experience of removing or reducing stress from life.

*How will you sell it? Promotion*

The marketing communication strategies and techniques all fall under the promotion heading. These may include advertising, sales promotions, special offers and public relations. Whatever the channel used, it is necessary for it to be suitable for the product, the price and the end user it is being marketed to. It is important to differentiate between marketing and promotion. Promotion is just the communication aspect of the entire marketing function.

How will you promote your services and products so that you reach your people? Do they hang out locally and find out about meetings in a certain way or online and hang out on certain platforms? How will you let them know that your doors are open when you launch? Are we throwing a giant party and emailing your list the custom invite or are you planning repeated get-togethers and rely on word of mouth organic growth? Many in my customer base are not near me so we talk a lot online, I need to be able to serve their needs from afar and still have them feel just as connected as the neighbor I bring cookies to. They need to be able to get to know who I am and what I am up to as much as I need to know how to advocate for them to social media is a large presence in my marketing plan.

If we continue to picture the building analogy, I am setting the design for the space. What's the color scheme? What type of tables? DO I want people to get in and get out or sit and settle? Imagine inside those walls I have posters with my wifi password so they can connect with friends and share online how much they like to hang out. I am also putting together a blog that they can read tips about how to remove the stress that they can share and promote their favorite place to hang out. You are filling the walls with the daily specials, a local volunteer opportunity board, and a calendar of special events. This step is focused on bringing people in and getting people to linger longer or share.

*Where will you sell it? Place*

Place or placement has to do with how the product will be provided to the customer. Distribution is a key element of placement. The placement strategy will help assess what channel is the most suited to a product. How a product is accessed by the end user also needs to complement the rest of the product strategy.

Where are you located and set up shop? Is it a great website shop and blog or an actual location in your house and in town? Do you have a booth at the farmers market all summer or setting up repeated meetings at a local coffee shop? Where are you staking your flag so people can find you? Many in my customer base shop local markets and like seasonal ingredients on their table and in their skincare. I need to recognize that in my audience and make sure I am partnered with similar values.

Ok so we built the walls, started planning the events, this step is focused on local and location. Have I reached out to other businesses on the same street that have similar interests and added in info? Maybe offered space for meetings? Have you started an after school special for kids and parents needing a place to study? Have you connected with the community yet? Imagine I set the scene for this business on Pinterest and I set up contracts with vendor events or the local farmers market for multiple years so I can be somewhere consistently and treat it as a popup. I have team meetings in similar places also so that becomes a 'known' place. You get involved locally and the business promotes complimentary services to local organizations so that way you build a community.

*How much is it? Price*

Price covers the actual amount the end user is expected to pay for a product. How a product is priced will directly affect how it sells. This is linked to what the perceived value of the product is to the customer rather than an objective costing of the product on offer. If a product is priced higher or lower than its perceived value, then it will not sell. This is why it is imperative to understand how a customer sees what you are selling. If there is a positive customer value, then a product may be successfully priced higher than its objective monetary value. Conversely, if a product has little value in the eyes of the consumer, then it may need to be underpriced to sell. Price may also be affected by distribution plans, value chain costs and markups and how competitors price a rival product.

Let's chat about affordability vs quality in concentration. Many people will tell me that they need a certain price point but also will spend way more if they get a great deal on a bundle that will last them months. It goes back to understanding the people around you and what they are willing to pay and what they are willing to buy. I know for a fact that ingredients are a big deal to mine. They will pay more for a company acts responsibly and pays people well. They respect companies that are good to animals, locally based, support women and minority-owned outreach, and provide a strong train to help people move out of poverty. They will spend a larger amount if the impact is there.

Ok so to continue our visual, we have walls, promotions, we designed the space, and connected locally. This is the step where we are either offering specials to frequent customer OR when we set the price of our products based on the other coffee shops or businesses around the corner. You want to see if your quality of product vs the price point already set for that area puts you in a reasonable range. Imagine that I make sure that I teach my customers how to navigate my website to easily get the best deal every time so they always feel like sharing. This adds convenience and quality to your product pricing. I make sure I have a VIP rewards group and offer deals just for those that are repeat customers. This helps reduce the price so it is more affordable. I recognize they may also be shopping for their family and need bulk order assistance or gift help during the holidays. This makes it easy to share and economical. Once this is decided, it is up to the customer to decide if it will be accepted.

*What do you sell? Products and services*

The product is either a tangible good or an intangible service that seems to meet a specific customer need or demand. All products follow a logical product life cycle and it is vital for marketers to understand and plan for the various stages and their unique challenges. It is key to understand those problems that the product is attempting to solve. The benefits offered by the product and all its features need to be understood and the unique selling proposition of the product need to be studied. In addition, the potential buyers of the product need to be identified and understood.

What you sell is going to be just as important as who buys it, where you are, how much it is, and how you talk about it. If you sell a bag of junk, you can say anything you want but you will not have people return to you. You will lose the trust you built in all the other steps as fast as a hair stylist that sells cheap products just to increase the amount of money spent in their salon. You want to respect the person you see you are taking care of and go out and find the best you can get. Considering the people around you and all the other steps, find the thing that fits perfectly and that makes you feel passionate.

Ok so to complete this space, you have built the walls, set up the design, connected with your location, promoted it to the customers, and set a price. Now if we are a restaurant, we craft a menu. If we are a bakery, we start selecting the main case items that will always be available. If you are in Direct Sales, we are stocking the shelves with the products or focusing on product knowledge. You are studying the actual products that your company offers and you are paying close attention to the services offered to hosts and teammates. Don't just sell the creams, sell the dreams.

*How do I pick a company or product to sell?*

Pay attention to trends and determine a niche market that makes sense. If you have never baked a cupcake in your life and you claimed online to be a chef you are not being genuine. If you tell them you are in school and experimenting with a new career they want to follow. If you start a skincare business with bad skin, show them your journey and let them follow along don't act like a sudden expert with zero experience.

*How do I pick a sponsor in Direct Sale OR a partner if I am build-*

*ing a storefront business?*

People often ask how do you pick a sponsor in Direct Sales. Many join a family member purely because they are the first they have found that are with that brand. Some join with a friend and later a family member joins and things get awkward at dinner or people have trouble picking between friends. Here is my official stance on this and you can completely ignore it if you need: pick a company you love, and a leader you can grow with. If your family or friend are just starting out, that can be a big benefit as you grow together. If you have the ability and know you need someone that is not a family member or friend to do well, make that choice so you can grow. The one thing I will never say is that the leader dictates the teammate's success. You can pick the most successful person ever and not work out. You can pick the most inexperienced and build something massive. The only thing in both settings is you, you have to be able to do the work to be successful either way. Pick the situation that will help you grow the best.

The same goes with building a partnership in a traditional business. Just because that person is family, doesn't mean they are loyal to your ideas like you are, responsible enough to manage money or taxes, or kind under pressure and nice to employees. Again, there are entire series of reality shows just focused on showing how harmful it is to have to work with family or friends that drive you nuts. Be cautious and careful with who you decide to build a business with.

## Launch your DIRECT SALES business Challenge

1. **Begin by purchasing the starter kit from a trusted sponsor.** (Product)

2. **While you wait for your kit to arrive,** start a list of 25 friends and family that you have seen purchase the type of items on the way. (Promotion)

3. **Set up an event or group with basic info about who you are, what you sell, and your weblink.** I also suggest the first post be a post about why your are selling these products. Doesn't have to be long: "At first I felt that...", "then I found ....", "now I feel..." is one way to create a simple statement about why you are doing this. (Place)

4. **Start making posts on your social using the products that you are preparing to sell**, inviting people to an exclusive event or group if they ask how to get them. (Promotion)

5. **When they ask you about how to buy it also, private message them or call/text them(do not roll your eyes, yes I said CALL).** Reach out and find out if they have ever tried your line and would they give you honest feedback. You want people to try something and then tell you if they like the products so if you can sample something out, send that. If you can not, ask if you can come over for coffee or send out a small item before the event starts. Include them as a product tester.(Promotion)

6. **Start adding people into the group and**

**message each with a google form to find out basics.** You can google how to create one very fast. Start with basic contact info including address, email, and phone. On the form make sure you ask if they want a catalog, to hold an event, and info on joining. This way even if you are scared to ask, it gets asked. Based on the company you are with questions can vary about cooking, soap, cleaning the house, nails, pets. Make sure the questions on this form help you to get to know the person that is interested so you can tailor the customer experience to them while you are launching. (Product/Price)

7. **Of the 25 people you connect with in step 2, there is a strong possibility that 1/3 will ignore you completely.** However many you need to push for, complete the 25 names. You want

25 people in this group when you launch. I like to pay attention also to the enthusiasm. If I have 5 people extremely excited you are doing great. So reach out to your personal cheerleaders and make sure they are all in. Then reach out to 1-5 people that have knowledge in this area also and will be expert witness to the quality. Maybe add in 1-5 people that are experienced with Direct Sales parties or have sold for a company also. 1-5 should be local, 1-5 maybe out of your area. (Place/Promotion)

8. **Connect:** you want something set up online, something in the mail, something in their texts, and maybe a calendar invite on the phone. In the age of people running fast, promotions are essential to launch.(Promotion)

9. **The day of the event**, if it is in person serve

light snacks. If it is online, make sure you triple check people are attending also. People will cancel so always have a plan for "If you missed it". I bundle up samples or send over a container of snacks and info to locals and they can look at the info from their own home. (Product/Promotion/Place). If they are out of town I get a bundle of info in the mail the same day so it arrives a few days later while the event is still on their mind.

10. **Rock the event.** Things are going to happen, you are going to say awkward stuff, and maybe no one will show. It is more important that you held the event vs the success. Learn from whatever happens and re attack. If it goes amazing, write down the major successes and repeat those. Attempt to get 3 events booked

from each event you hold. This way if 1 in 3 cancel you are still building momentum.

# Congrats! You just launched your business!!

# CHAPTER 4
# NO SHE DOESN'T
No, she doesn't know how to help customers and not be spammy.

..................................................

I stood there with sweaty palms holding out a sample. "Here is a sample for you to try!" (gulp) "Can I...would you...um...what is your email, phone number, address, and blood type?" Ok, maybe I didn't ask their blood type when I handed out samples but I am confident it felt like it when I handed them my google form, giveaway entry form, or whatever I was trying to use to get as much info as possible.

I have always had trouble asking people for what I really needed and believing they would trust me with that info. I have learned how to be very careful with consumer information from working on a military base, working at Delta, and working at Disney. I know what can go wrong with a check and how bad it is if you do not use information responsibly. I also have friends and family that will not use their credit cards online and will not read them out over the phone. It is a hard balance to lead a business halfway across the US when you have security concerns about consumer information being handled correctly.

So over the last 20 years in sales, I have learned that there is power in asking for the information and just as much power when someone answers. Anyone that has been spammed with unwanted emails, texts, and phone calls runs in fear from people with bad intentions.

Something I am sensitive to, I have good intentions but I am in sales. People judge salespeople as vultures and ugly because some make very poor choices. I can only hold myself accountable for what I can control, I can control how I show my customer that I am worthy of their info.

I am a people person at heart. I care about their comfort and get concerned about how they view me. Many have assumed it comes from me trying to benefit in shady ways because I have anxiety, and anxiety makes you awkward as heck. I will look nervous in situations that shouldn't require fear. I will also say random jokes to kill dead air and make small talk. When I started with Disney I had a meeting with a manager that basically revolved around me needing to take a sip of water after asking scary sales questions because I had to stop talking to hear people saying YES! I was so scared of people saying no I wouldn't let them speak! That is the same as asking someone on a date and TALKING ALL THE WAY THROUGH THE ANSWER! Stop being so scared! I have had to learn that I will get concerned in settings that are silly and convince myself they have already decided not to give me the info I need! So I will stand there in fear when in reality I am giving a person looking for info was to actually get it! They want it! I need to be able to connect and contact those that are interested in my products.

In sales, customer information is the food and water to your business. You need new customers and the data is the proof that they are interested in finding out more. If it is good data you can find them anywhere. If it is bad or fractured data you can only find them a few certain ways and that is not the best way to build a relationship.

Ponder this: My grandfather was great at sales in the 60s/70s. He used to know that a phone number or business card in your Rolodex could be a lifetime of sales. For the young, a Rolodex is cards with contact info in a box or on a circular, rotating file device used to store business contact information. As a salesperson, you could take your Rolodex from job to job and sustain a good income as long as you chose products to sell that your customers needed and your customers would remain loyal to you. It was kind of like your value as a salesperson.

Big Rolodex, big following.

In 2019 and beyond, your customer and email list are your power. If you are thinking small, you can email customers and reach them as long as they check it. If you are beginning to think big, you have a name and email you can find that person on almost any social media, and that is where the biggest win happens. Let's say you have a large following on a certain social platform, you can now find them again if that media closes up. This keeps your business going long after the first product or company you are with is gone or shuttered! Your brand build value. It is your value to advertisers because you can use emails to increase your follower count. Imagine if you took your email list for your company right now, have you taken full advantage of this info and

## This Doesn't Make Me An Expert

found your customers where they hang out the most? Are you going to them and learning about what they share, like, post, promote, invest in, laugh about, and who they are friends with also? Are you getting to know the people that want to know more about you? Are you getting to know their life as much as you expect them to know you? A great leader said people buy from people they know, like, and trust. Can you say that is happening in your business?

If your answer is no, let's get to work!

*Start with 'Good' data on every customer.*

### GOOD DATA IS:
### NAME /ADDRESS/EMAIL/PHONE

From that, you can reach out in real life by

sending goodies, outside of social by texting or calling, and you can use the email to find them on social media. This info also helps you to start following up effectively. You are not relying on a single message after your launch that goes unread, you can reach out in a few ways before assuming that you are being rejected. This is a part of business that many shy away from because they do not want to feel pushy. When I need to remember that I am not bothering people, I remind myself that they gave me all this info so I could get in touch. People are very busy, remember that when you are messaging and getting discouraged. People will tell you if they want you to go away.

Now that we have launched(or relaunched depending on your situation), you can sort new customers based on where they are in knowing about your business, this is called a Sales Funnel. Many discuss sales funnels in spammy ways so be careful how you work this idea. The idea of this is to NOT force people through the steps, it is helping them learn more if they are interested. A customer SHOULD NEVER know where you believe they are in this section. This is for you. You want to focus the most time on people that love what you do and understand why you are doing it!

*What is it?*

In this step, no one knows who you are or recognizes your logo or products. You are starting from scratch! Do you remember life before knowing what a bath bomb was? Maybe it is the step that you went through the weeks leading up to you finding a new restaurant in your neighborhood. What about how life felt before you knew Instagram or Snapchat existed. You don't know what you are missing but also, you aren't missing it. It is not in your consciousness so you may have seen ads but don't remember them. That is why many experts call this the Awareness stage! This is when they visit your website or event for the first time, which the found from an ad, Google search, a post shared on social media, or another traffic source.

Your customer might also become aware of the problem that they need to solve and the possible ways to deal with it. They ask "What is xxx?" They have now noticed your logo, start interacting with your brand, and start learning you exist.

When I need to remind myself what it

feels like to be in this stage, I drive through a neighborhood in my town that I normally do not frequent. I need fresh eyes, I need to notice new stores. I need to notice the stores that may be new in my own area of town. I need to stumble upon a new store downtown. It is important that while you get immersed in your own branding, you understand the people that aren't there yet. It will help you to understand the needs of new people coming into view!

*Have you tried it?*

In this step, people recognize you exist but they do not have personal experience to share yet. They may have seen a few ads, maybe a friend tried it, and maybe they saw it in their store but didn't stop by it yet! At this point, they decide it is time to try it out! Welcome to the

Interest phase! Now is the time when they express interest in your product or service. They follow you on social media and subscribe to your list.

Your customer may show interest by asking for samples or coming to an event to try out the products. They may be following your posts and they may be waiting and watching. This is the best reason you should ALWAYS have something in your bag so that you can help people try out. You want to have something easy to share without needing a sales pitch or presentation.

When I need to remind my team of this stage, I tell teammates to go open up a new product from your company that you have not ever tried. I want you to pay close attention to how you pick the item you grab first! Is it the smell, the taste, the feel? Did you read the label? Did you go after certain colors or names? What is drawing you in? Then open it up, make the item, or put the item on. How does it feel? Notice how impactful the senses are in you being drawn into a consumable product or purchase! If it is food, how important is it to convey what the finished product tastes like? How important is that connection to trying something to understanding who you are as a company? Attempt to see the world through the eyes of someone that has tried something from you for the first time ever.

*Have you bought it?*

Ok, so we know you exist, we have tried it out, next, we need to decide to buy it! Your

Customer Prospect is making the decision that they want to take advantage of your solution. They are paying more attention to what you offer, including deals and options, so the can make the final decision to purchase. This is the step when sales offers are made by using bundling, rewards, benefits, and discounts.

Your customer has already built confidence that your product or service is a possible solution to their issue, but now they want to see options. I have never thought of the first time a person buys from me as a sale because it may go completely wrong, just as the first time they try my product they may not like that specific item. So I slow down at this stage, based on matching a need to a product causes a customer to really connect with your brand so that search may take a few tries. AND THAT IS OK! I go to a pizza place and try our a few versions before I decide that is my pizza place. I am focused on being the best consultant I can not the top salesperson. It is about the person so that needs to be person-focused. Yes, they are buying a product, but pay attention to the fact that your customer is deciding the PERSON to buy from also.

I always picture every purchase like it is a giant financial investment. Imagine if someone was looking at buying something from you like they do when they buy a car or house. Is it the right time? The right product? The right deal? The right features? What will make them jump in or walk away? What would make you or your family? What goes through your mind if someone tells you everything and overwhelms you? What happens if you feel like information is incomplete? What causes you to trust the person selling something to you and what causes you to back out of a deal? You can answer every question perfectly and not be the perfect person that they want to do business with. In other cases, people may pick you first. It can feel personal but don't make it that way. All of these thoughts can help you feel confident in understanding how someone else is deciding if you have the right item or opportunity for them! Use the perspective to find the next person!

*Have you shared it?*

Many assume that a sale is the end of the funnel for sales transactions, you have lied to yourself and given up WAY too soon. Follow my line of thought: I can sell a person 1,000 products in a bulk order and that is spectacular, or I can sell a person 1 product every year and they share it with 1,000 people. Then those 1,000 share it with one more person, and every year my business will be stronger because a person loyal enough to share will be a bigger deal connecting customers to other customers than any print advertising dollar. Word of mouth pays out the largest and most consistent Return On Investment every time. It all boils down to people looking out for people instead of corporations telling people what to buy, at that point we are back at TRUST. I personally set goals on how well my brand is shared instead of just on how much someone buys. It will also RUIN your business if you suck, but that is a different chapter. Right now, we are in the Sharing part of this funnel and it is about to get inspiring. Stay focused.

If you are in direct sales, this is the moment they beg you for a party so they can make sure their friends hear all about it. Just kidding, that barely happens for some people, so let's talk about reality. Yes, many see this as hosting a party or an event. But more likely this is the moment you may not ever see, it is the moment they buy a gift from your website for a family member during the holidays or share your link. This could be a social media post at your store about that t-shirt with the witty quote. This is the blog post that goes viral because an influencer found your purse 'on brand'. This may also be the moment that a cousin tags you below a post online asking for recommendations or solutions, especially if you have a local storefront! It is the moment they recommend your cakes for a birthday or order lunch for co-workers. It can also be the day they invite all their friends to their dinner at your restaurant or on vacation to your hotel! It is the moment they need others to also see what they have found! Are you getting the picture? It is that important moment when it goes from a personal purchase to a group experience. This is the stage you find out if you are not just a product to buy, but an experience to share.

Have you ever taken a bite of something and immediately decided a person next to you was required to also taste it? Italians are not the only people to do this. I have seen Jews, Hispanics, and almost every mother do this to their families. It is the scoop of ice cream, the slice of cake, the small of a flower, the new candle. That is sharing! You are so passionate about the experience you are having that you can not even consider that someone would not feel the same way and you refuse to keep them from living life without it. I have seen this with skincare, food, music, and makeup. It becomes infectious and exciting. You run around and pull people into your moment. You feel it from your toes and you have to share. It becomes an instinct to find things worth sharing, this is when you start to see your own influence over friends. One buys the lipstick, we all buy the lipstick. You pick and chose what gets spotlighted. It is not a constant line of saying the same thing over and over like a copy and paste description, it is a passionate response to your mind expanding rapidly. That is how they feel when they fall in love with your brand and your products. They can not contain themselves.

*Will you sell it?*

This is a critical, and often expensive, step that many get into. You find this amazing product or service, it is easy to share and suddenly you see money because all your friends are buying it up because you told them it was awesome! I have seen this happen from one plate of cupcakes being devoured at a church picnic and suddenly the person is thousands of dollars in debt because they thought everyone liked their cupcakes! This happens often in many industries, I even had a woman in Orlando tell me she started a skincare line because she wanted her name on a bottle. Not because she loved skincare, but because she liked seeing people holding things that had her name. I was not surprised by the ugly ingredients and poor manufacturing because she could have cared less about what was inside. That is like decorating cakes and hating to bake the cake part. Just don't. Full STOP. The step we are entering is the moment when sharing is not enough, it is when you are wanting to SELL this product and turn it into a business. You can see that there is a need in the market(demand) and feel the product or service can answer the need while being profitable(supply).

A Direct Sales customer considering joining your company or a person that likes your franchise enough to ask about how to build something like yours acts way differently than a person that just likes sharing. There is a different pace and purpose to the questions they start to ask. They start to work on a bigger decision process than a person interested in spending $20-50, these choices are based on how much time they want to invest and large financial choices like inventory, advertising, income information, and profitability. In Direct Sales, the conversation about a kit can go a few directions on the surface but it is your job to decipher what is really being discussed. Opportunity. While some join for the discount on items, because that discount as stated above can help a new teammate make a sale. While some say they just want to connect with friends, they want to know if people are interested in trying stuff and sticking around. Some will say they want a small income to pay a bill, which is basically asking how consistent your sales are. The biggest is if they ask if your company trains you on how to really work this business. That is the same as asking a franchise owner if the original store will teach them how to be successful and will there be continued support as they grow and hit harder challenges. That is a person that COULD build a business for life if given the correct resources. Understanding how all of these customers fit helps you understand how to help them get started strong, which then impacts how they maintain. But they need to have the passion to drive their own success.

A while ago I made a joke to a friend that I should open a business that delivers martinis, this friend responded by asking me if I wanted to open that business or shop from that business. This is a question many people do not get from their circles when opening a DS or traditional business. Do you want to sell xxx or buy xxx? Because if you get into business purely because you wanted to buy an xxx, you are about to lose your savings account. You will ignore important moments like taxes, accounting, and payroll or you will lose all passion for xxx because of ugly employees that take the fun out of life. It happens all over and that is why they have reality TV shows to film it for entertainment. When I want to remind myself what it feels like to want to sell something so badly you can't contain yourself, I go and consider how I sell my products and why I am here. Why are you doing this? Do you love the look in the face of a mom that learned to cook? Are you excited when you see a new box of product show up because as you open the box you picture the lives that are about to change with the new fragrance? Does helping a dad find the perfect gift for Mother's Day flower bundle cause your heart to blow up? Do you love what you do even when you are sitting in front of the Quickbooks spreadsheets? Do you understand that even "the boring" cleaning of the kitchen is as important, if not more, as the fun cupcake specials? You can hate parts of stuff, but it is all worth it to get to see a teammate succeed or feeling like you are making the world better by opening your door in the morning. Even when it is hard. Even when no one is cheering. Even when you have to do the tasks that aren't fun as a hobby. Even when no one believes in your dream.

## WORKING WITH CUSTOMERS

A long time ago my grandmother took me

## This Doesn't Make Me An Expert

for ice skating lessons. The first time on the ice they teach you how to fall down so you hurt yourself less when it happens because it is going to happen. I think this lesson sunk into my brain for a lot of reasons as I grew up because change is inescapable, failure is going to happen, and how fast you are to get up is determined by how big the bruise is on your butt. I have had big ugly bruises in life and some have come from moments like my first time on the phones for Disney Reservations.

My first phone call at Disney caused me to sob because I could not tell a woman the time of a parade nearly a year out. I had been logged in for under a minute and it was the first person I had ever talked to as a Cast Member. I was mortified when the calendar info stopped working

6 months out and I had to say "I am sorry, I don't seem to have that info." The woman unloaded on me as if I had just canceled her vacation by hitting the wrong button on the computer. It was terrifying and I immediately logged off.

So to save you from similar situations I am going to teach you something that has helped me ever since I worked for Starbucks. LATTE. Listen, Acknowledge, Thank, Take Action, Encourage. It was a major piece of knowledge that caused Delta and Disney to be way more enjoyable. I knew how to communicate effectively with a person that was about done with me being in front of them.

Listen to what they have to say, Disney also recommended asking clear questions so you know exactly what you are working with. This also helped me while I was selling a vacation. Listening shouldn't need to be listed when dealing with customers BUT it is the step that can prevent everything else from going WAY WAY worse.

Acknowledge and checking for understanding tend to go hand in hand. Confirming you not just heard what they were saying but you also understand where their mind it helps people feel heard after you may have asked questions for a few minutes. I even do this with the kids and husband: Do I understand that you are currently mad because the guy in the video game shot the other guy in the video game and you feel like throwing the controller as revenge?

Thanking a person that is yelling at you requires you to check in with yourself first. Are you using the correct tone and facial expressions? There is a big difference in smiling "Thank you so much for your feedback, Ma'am." And yelling "THANK YOU FOR YOUR FEEDBACK, MA'AM" Most certainly it can also make a difference between employed and totes not. So start by thanking a person sincerely for giving you the opportunity to solve the issue or thank them for being a loyal customer. People like to be thanked for basically anything because not many do it well anymore. Use that to your advantage and make sure they understand that you actually appreciate them not staying silent. Silence can cost you a lot more money while you guess why your customers have disappeared. So thank them for letting you handle the issue on site and at the moment! If this is just a normal day, thank the person for being patient or loving the products or services you offer as much as you do! Thank them for investing in your business or just for coming in today!

Take action can seem simple until you get the wrong burger after all the other steps. Ideally, if you listened well, confirmed details, and knew what to thank them for you really should know how to take action. Go solve the problem...find the zit creme, fix the order, change the reservation, adjust the order. Just do it. If there is red tape, find a way to solve it without them needing to ask as a courtesy. You are working on behalf of your customer or guest, treat them how you would want you to be treated. That also means, triple check the bag you are about to hand them, make sure you know what they will need to do in 5 steps or less, and make things easy by adding in anything they would need.

You have rocked out listening, acknowledging, thanking them, and taking action. Last is encouraging! This can be encouraging them to speak to a supervisor so they have better options, encouraging them to email corporate so they have feedback, or encouraging them to return again because you love their face. It is really that simple.

Serving customers can be overwhelming and scary, especially when you are gathering info and trying to help them. Basically anytime and always. But remember, the majority of your customers are either friends and family or they love what you are doing. They want you to succeed because you help them and their friends with a solution. Stay focused on that and be considerate along the way. If you love this job, you know this is not about just getting a sale, but a lifetime of fulfilling a need.

*Fun Facts:*

\*80 % of your time will be spent on customers that have tried your product, bought your product, shared your business as a host or loyalty, or joined your team. 20% will be focused on new customers learning you exist!

\*If you are a team leader the stats start to divide with 60% of the 80% as customer focused, 20% will now be brand team teammates getting started. That last 20% will be teammates that are confidently able to be independent. Very similar to in a restaurant, 60% will be focused on the guests eating and sharing, 20% on new hires learning how to serve, and then 20% on the rest of the staff running independently.

*1 person will tell 1-5 people if they love something about your business, 1 person will tell 10-20(or more now with social) if something goes wrong with your business.

*Of the people that actually make it all the way through the funnel to actually join your team or open a franchise, statistically speaking 1-2 out of 5 will actually make this into a big empire. 1-2 will also either sell nothing or fail before even launching. The largest group is often inconsistent and not the highest in sales on your team or in your business. All of these people are important lessons on leadership. Consider the people that joined and never sold practice so you are strong for when those that can make it big as you scary questions. Consider those that are independent and hit high goals to be your real workers. Consider the majority your stability and motivation while you build. Everyone has a place on the team.

### EMAIL LIST CHALLENGE

**1. Start by figuring out the best way to see your customer data.** Many use free spreadsheets and some pay for software. It all depends on your level of income, you can start with free. Make sure for every customer you have all the data we discussed.

-You can then start putting it into action by

finding friends on all media.

-You can also pick an email service and begin to build a list that you can market to when we talk about social media.

2. **If you have a calendar full of "events"**( parties, one on ones, networking meetings, webinars, calls…it all counts), consider which build up current customer bases vs building a new base:

-If you are doing parties with the exact same people at all the locations, those are reorders.

-If you have each person bring a new friend next time you turn this into a balanced event.

-If you have an entire calendar of events focused on new customers, balance by adding in events for loyal customers.

-If you are starting out, stick to the percentages so that you are treating your customers you are gaining so well they help you with word of mouth advertising and start helping you fill your calendar.

## CHAPTER 5
## NO SHE SHOULDN'T
No, she shouldn't create her own
brand and marketing plan.

........................................................

One of the hardest parts of building your brand is self-acceptance. Learning that who you are and believing that persona deserves to be loved is an integral part of branding. Accepting that who you are is worthy of building a following in life and online is something no one talks about. Because it is never discussed, many never realize that you can dictate what you share and people will follow you through fire because they see you are genuine.

Many want to tell you all about who you are in your life. Your parents, your friends, and other influencers are working through lenses that could put their own fears and concerns for how you will turn out onto you before you even have the chance to reflect on what you want from your life and business. Changing that opinion can be almost impossible because it is ingrained in moments where you hear things like "Why aren't you like.." "But you have to (insert preconceived idea) to be successful and stable in life."

The plan is to erase that, I want you to be yourself and come to the table proud of who you are, flaws and all. The real brand is your flaws, the cracks in a persona. It is relatable! For example, I am comfortable in PJs and bathrobes. I teach people to take off the makeup that causes perfection and show them that a bare face is nothing to fear. My brand tells you that rawness and imperfection is a strength.

So how did I turn that realness into a brand: be yourself. Find your own interests and incorporate genuine aspects. You don't have to subscribe to 100% of a catalog to be yourself, just like a chef doesn't eat every item on their menu. You have to live your life and add your products or services in where it makes sense to your audience. Being unnatural about why you are sharing your products creates distrust. They want to see who you are, why they want to hear from you, and why they want to see what you are going to do next. You have to also build yourself up to be ready to grow and be vocal about your passions. Just like we discussed customers needing to be willing to share, recognize that passion has to continue into selling.

## Cupcakes

My first experience with personal branding came from a nonprofit business I built very quickly in North Dakota in the middle of the winter. I loved making cakes but it was expensive. I started with making food for Dave to bring to work and around December of 2009, I walked into an Obstetrics appointment and was told that I was going to need to not have any more babies after the one I was pregnant with because they were concerned about repeated C-Sections. I am 85% sure this doctor was full of crap after a few more months of bad info but at this moment I had very clue how to process this, so I started baking, it was therapy.

The first real project with cupcakes happened Jan 2010 with Cupcakes for Haiti after the first earthquake. I created flavors that were basics and a couple of fun items, I asked a manager if I could set up in the break room at Delta Vacations and sold out in a single lunch. All the funds were put into my account and I donated it all to the United Nations Food Program that was the best option for donating at the time. I then had a friend who owned a wine bar ask if I could make her some also and she sold out the first set also. This was gaining major momentum.

Sara was born happy and healthy in New Jersey in June 2010 as I was launching my cupcake business in North Dakota after leaving Delta Vacations. I was so excited to bring her home a couple days after having her but it was harder making the bigger cakes and breastfeed. By the time I was back up on my feet after another c-section, I had a full calendar of cakes and cupcakes!

The cupcakes Dave kept bringing into work caused many to really pay attention. I also felt like I could mess with great combos and no one was making cupcakes like this in town. The flavor pairings I was creating while I was pregnant came from cravings and wishing I could just have a mojito or baileys. I was craving toasted PB & j and that turned into an amazing cupcake. I was also learning how to do stuff from cookbooks my grandfather had left me with little guidance. I made a mistake with buttercream and it looked like ice cream when I scooped it so I made cupcakes that looked like ice cream sundaes. It was awesome! I was inspired and focused!

Sasha Sweder

In Jan 2011, Dave had a training opportunity in Alabama and I told him we were all coming. I know this didn't seem exciting to him to stuff his entire family into a one bedroom hotel but I actually look back and find it to be a pivotal point for me mobilizing people back home. One night I was thinking about how everyone gives away stuff to shelters for Thanksgiving and Christmas, but ignore Valentine's Day. What if we could do something awesome for families that had survived domestic violence for the holiday all about love? I posted the idea online to a military spouse group and people WENT NUTS. I started knitting scarves and it escalated fast to 33 baskets of magic, clothes, food, treat, and everything we could get our hands on. I would sit in the childcare room knitting until my hands fell off hoping I could have basic hats and scarves for 33 baskets. By the time we got home, we had enough stuff for a homeless shelter and the domestic violence shelter to fill 5 cars. It was amazing and moving to the people involved. When we dropped it all off there was a moment where everyone turned and looked at me and asked what was next. My heart stopped, I had no clue.

In Feb 2011 Sara was already almost a year and becoming more independent, the funding for the Deployed Spouse group dried up and they used to have meals monthly for people with their spouses overseas. It was perfect for the same group of people to take action! I refused to believe we couldn't do something so I started baking. I believe I made about 10 dozen and started talking to a bunch of businesses downtown, my friends and I stood outside of multiple businesses selling cupcakes and collecting donations until we could pay for 25 spouses to have manicures and pedicures for Valentine's Day.

I loved having the ability to help them so much that I started to help Squadrons volunteer to cover each monthly meetings and when they couldn't I sold cupcakes to cover it.

People started to really follow what I was doing, but more so, the team that would jump in. In 2011, Minot ND had a 500-year flood cripple their town. The same exact group took action! We were making food, sandbagging, mobilizing social media, and gathering our community around what needed to happen. If you have never walked into a Shoppette and filled an entire fleet of cars with beverages or cooked for 165 National Guard from a 4 burner kitchen, I suggest you give it a try. It makes you feel like you can help the world.

People knew who we were and they knew my cupcakes tasted good and supported good things. That was my brand. People would tag me in every picture of a cupcake and every cupcake joke on the internet, but my brand was how I made them feel when those cupcakes paid for help in the community.

When I started with my direct sales business I needed to sit down and analyze why people felt so confident sharing and investing in those cupcakes. They believed in me, they believed in the impact, and they believed they were part of a community. That is also what you can do with yours. Here is how!

*A brand is more than a logo*

The definition on Google when you search for the definition of "brand" is a type of product manufactured by a particular company under a particular name. Branding is defined as the promotion of a particular product or company by means of advertising and distinctive design. Both contribute to how people can recognize you for what you stand for, what you say, what you are selling, and your story. Your brand is how people will see you and interact with you as a business. You can take the name Sasha Sweder and see only the person, or you can see the brand Sasha Sweder as the business. Sasha Sweder runs after children, shops for groceries in the tub, and loves weekends at the movies eating nachos. Sasha Sweder the brand is up late with cups of coffee after dinner or a martini looking for new people to inspire to build an empire. I believe that my brand has her act together: she is the person that cleans, folds, and puts her laundry away in one day. A magical unicorn of unrealistic and focused fabulousness. That being said, you are going to need one. We cover that in the challenge.

*Develop the bigger picture.*

YOU are the main part, not the products you sell. Think about going to a hair salon, you are the owner. People know you for who you are and what you stand for. You are creating the setting for your brand to perform. You design the storefront, then hire the people that will participate in the goals of the brand. We use content and character to create the services those people provide. We merchandise that brand and that experience with your products so your community can bring that experience home. So in our analogy, you are at the point of the blank white walls. Your spirit should be so integral to the foundation and walls that no one could consider replicating what you build inside.

Example:

This year I was finally old enough to actually brand my name. I have fought against this name since I was young, I loved my last name more than my name for a few more years. There is Sasha the mom, Sasha the wife, Sasha the daughter, Sasha the sister, Sasha the leader. I needed to feel whole and less compartmentalized. This is the first time in a while I feel empowered by who Sasha is. It needed to be my name, and it needed to be the whole thing.

**Colors:**

-Go look at what you are already building and see color trends. A great place to see this is Pinterest boards. We are looking for three colors. Start with the main color that will be the most prominent, then a secondary color perfect for text colors or less seen. Always have a neutral that can be used in pops of focus: black, brown, white or navy.

-Do you have superstitions? I have a strong belief that what surrounds you can remind you of your goals. When people on my team tell me they plan to hit the top of our company, I make sure silver is in everything they are working on. I want you to see that color with your name every day and believe that is coming. Drive yourself to it. So if you want a blue car and you can only get that car when you hit it big, that logo should have blue in it. It can be chalked up to silliness but it works on many levels.

-Do you also understand the power of colors in advertising in your industry?

*Red is associated with passion and love but its strong intensity also signifies excitement, determination, and courage.

*Orange is also a dynamic and energetic color but doesn't have the danger overtones conveyed by red. It draws attention to itself for its lively nature and can be used successfully for modern adverts that want to stand out.

*Yellow is bright, reminiscent of the sun and full of energy. It also signifies playfulness, amusement, curiosity, and happiness making it an ideal color choice for advertising children's activities. Darker yellows, bordering on gold, can give a feeling of prosperity and security.

*Green is firmly linked with nature and the environment in most people's minds. It is also associated with reliability, safety, stability, honesty, and freshness.

*Blue is a color which arouses trust in the viewer. It may be a little serious, but it also suggests success, depth, loyalty, calmness, and power.

*Purple is associated with luxury, royalty, dreams, mystery, and elegance. Light can be calming like lavender, dark can feel glam and indulgent.

*Pink is sweet, young and vulnerable. It will

always be associated with femininity at a subconscious level.

*Browns ranging from mid beiges to chocolate browns lend themselves nicely to advertising for niche markets where brown is a dominant color such as coffee and chocolate manufacturers, and pet services.

*Black, white, & white showcase traditionalism, conservatism and neutrality, and can be used very effectively in advertising. Organizations that want to portray themselves as completely trustworthy and serious will succeed well with these neutrals!

Example:
SashaSweder.com blog is grey, blush pink, white with pops of green. Grey for my goals, pink for my heart feeling vulnerable, white for

purity of the future and green for the growth.

**Theme:**

Advertising theme is when you create a central, repetitive message that promotes brand awareness and is meant to provide an impact beyond just individual or disconnected ads. A theme of advertising is a central idea intended to trigger the desired action from customers. Take a moment to think about a friend that is known for repeated posting or tagging about baths, food, sparkles, animals, or an object like bikes. It is memorable and recognizable because you are conditioned from seeing that theming. If done authentically you will see that theme everywhere you go. For example, once I decided that my theme for my blog was going to have succulent plants, I noticed I already had them all over the house and shopped looking for more ways to add them in.

For SashaSweder.com I chose coffee cups and succulents, I am known to be over-caffeinated in a coffee shop coming up with ideas. I also lose my coffee mugs all over the house after my brain squirreling off. Succulents make me think of low maintenance life that is strong. They come in different colors and can be easy for anyone to approach and add in. They defy the odds and look like whatever the heck they want. They don't have to take up much space but remain gorgeous.

**Know Your Audiences:**

My worlds have always felt scattered online. There was a time where my life was all food all the time. There was another phase that was a military spouse to the maximum. The next was all Direct Sales and Disney. While I could see that I was the bridge, I could never speak to all of them at once and show that the audience actually did have connections and things in common. In the Branding challenge, you will start to see that the person that wants to discuss movies for hours with you can also understand your products and services if you explain why you saw it as a need. You have the ability to connect audiences the way you connected your worlds. It all takes knowing your bubbles of interests, hobbies, and friends enough to give them great content and a way to create a community. While one may have thought to only have a single topic blog or social media, by not including all of your friends and family you miss out on the connections and they miss out on building a community.

Example: My food community loves my food blogs because I talk about indulgent ways to spoil yourself that include cheese one week but may involve face mask with wine themes the next. By showing how wine can be the connection between my foodies and my bath ladies, the world opens up for both bubbles on why they both love me so much.

## BRANDING CHALLENGE

1. **Grab a piece of paper.** Put the words I AM in the center of the page in a circle.

2. **Put a circle that branches off that says either ME or SELF.** Next, a branch and bubble that says Spouse/GF/BF. Another circle if you have kids(one for each if you have more than one).

Another for work, school, associations, each hobby, each interest.

3. **Then next to each circle you are going to get specific about circles that connects you...**for example, I am only a former military spouse because of my spouse so my husband gives me an authentic handshake into that world. Because of my daughter, I know what DIY crafts and Shopkins are. Because of my son, I have learned all about ADHD, ODD, and so much more about anxiety. Because of my summer camp, I know about sailing. Look for connections you personally have that mean things to you.

WHY: This chart is like a family tree of interests, references, social circles, and groups that can help you navigate creating a group of customers, join FB groups, booking parties, and even growing a super strong Frontline without saturating a circle with spam. It is the reason that not everyone can see me working all the time and how I manage to always have someone needing posh love. Based on the theme, these are our bubbles. No one will have the same chart, everyone will be unique, everyone has space to blossom into giant beautiful fishtanks of empires. Some may have crossovers but no one is exactly like you!

HOW: FROM THESE BUBBLES YOU CAN START A MORE ACCURATE AND DETAILED FRANKS LIST AND BRAND KEY THEMES. If you bounce from bubble to bubble with content on your social media, use these in your hashtags. Use this as the themes on your blog. When you're contacting people, pay attention so you figure out the Influencers in each bubble...you can add those Influencers to your Customers, Hosting List, or Frontlines. Set a goal to add one person from each bubble! An Influencer is a trusted and authentic friend willing to share to that bubble and when they start to sell they will be greeted with excitement for their new business or franchise. Have a Frontline from each bubble and your team will be selling to all your circles at once. This leaves you with room to grow as a person, as a brand, and still have access to all the groups! Boom.

4. Now grab a notebook. **Answer the following questions**:

-What is your company's mission?
-What are the benefits and features of your

products or services?

-What do your customers and prospects already think of your company?

-What qualities do you want them to associate with your company?

5. **Get a great logo.** Of course, logo design is just one small subset of branding, but the logo or brand mark remains the centerpiece of most branding schemes. Place it everywhere. You can look up apps and check reviews. Some well known apps are Canva, TailorBrands, Fiveer, Makr. Go based on the most updated options. I personally like apps I can do things myself and not pay a lot because I make changes a lot. Some will charge you up to $250 and some will not, so do your research before signing things. The apps I use tend to charge me around $6-10.

You want transparent png images so that you have the ability to use it all over the place and making things like professional. You can also look up a few types of logos like ones with word mark, brand mark, letter mark, or iconic logo. Do not get crazy but make it your own.

**If you are a traditional business owner, you want a logo for:**

-Your name/each partner and the name of your site(no .com) for emails or signing or letterhead and business cards

-The weblink(dot com) for social media outside the website

-The title of the business(like the sign on the store)

**If you are in DS:**

-Your name and website logo(use on social)

-Your name and the name of the site(No weblink for personalizing things like for emails or signing or letterhead and business cards)

-Your team name(similar name of the full business branding)

-The blog name (no .com for use on the site headers or info)

6. **Write down your brand messaging.** What are the key messages you want to communicate about your brand? Every employee should be aware of your brand attributes.

7. **Integrate your brand.** Branding extends to every aspect of your business--how you answer your phones, what you or your salespeople wear on sales calls, your e-mail signature, everything. I have even gone so far to go clothes shopping so that the clothing I am

wearing at meetings is part of my brand. I want to feel immersed when I walk up to someone new. It gives me confidence.

**8. Create a "voice" for your company that reflects your brand.** This voice should be applied to all written communication and incorporated in the visual imagery of all materials, online and off. Is your brand friendly? Be conversational. Is it ritzy? Be more formal. You get the gist. The most important part of being myself means I may have a tone, you know my tone. Picture that for you.

**9. Develop a tagline.** Write a memorable, meaningful and concise statement that captures the essence of your brand. People say that I say #JustSayin enough during videos that it is catchy. What do you say a lot? Be authentic.

10. **Design templates and create brand standards for your marketing materials.** Use the same color scheme, logo placement, look and feel throughout. You don't need to be fancy, just consistent. I absolutely loved doing this in Canva but there are many options. I was able to drill down to the color codes I wanted on all info, the fonts, and what I wanted party graphics to even look like. Another great resources on this is Pinterest boards we will create in the next chapter. Once we get that far, you will be able to create a visual of your branding and it will help you take it the next steps forward.

11. **Be true to your brand.** Customers won't return to you--or refer you to someone else-- if you don't deliver on your brand promise. Do

not restrict yourself, make your brand your house. You can recreate the color scheme as much as you want, but if the feel isn't right you will know. We want your brand to fit like a comfy shirt and the best room in your house. Your brand promise needs to also be a core value that you can do, not a big giant promise you struggle with. This is one of the rare moments I will say: brand promise should be heavily in your comfort zone.

12. **Be consistent.** I placed this point last only because it involves all of the above and is the most important tip I can give you. If you can't do this, your attempts at establishing a brand will fail. I am not the best at this but I have found tools like auto scheduling to help me do better. Being consistent creates comfort for

your team and your customers. If you struggle like I do, dedicate the energy to find the best ways. The time will be worth the pay out.

## CHAPTER 6
## NO, SHE COULDN'T.
### No, she couldn't learn how to professionally post online.

........................................................

Social media marketing is often talked about like you are doing the bare minimum by making posts and pretty pictures. It is nothing about pretty pictures and captions, it is about algorithms and statistics. It is connecting with people though a pretty post and a great caption that brings groups together to be social. If you think that a person that takes their info seriously did not consider the shade of the background and the shadow of the product, the potential to stop your scroll, the influence on the time of day on your perspective, and the amount of people that will view it so they get engagement you are ignoring a job that is claimed by many but actually done well by only a few.

Your brand that you built did not start with this business, it started when you were young and trying new things. Your brand comes to life when you live. If you make a new friend, learn a new hobby, get a new haircut, or fall in love with a song then your brand has expanded just like when you see an Influencer connect with a new product line. You connect people and that is what makes things social about what you are doing. The part you my be missing is that you have control over where and when that brand interacts with others. It is the reason people get scared to post about their business on their social media the first time, you are introducing new facts to people that already know you. They will either accept those facts or reject them and stop following. This is scary in a world dependent on likes and follows for validation.

## WHAT IF WE REMOVED THAT PRESSURE?

How? Let's shut the whole world down and picture a high school cafeteria. Let's imagine those great I AM bubbles as tables. You have a group of friends at each table and you have to chose to sit down at one table and feel insecure because you are worried that the other tables will up and leave. That is that fear you are feeling. Your business and all it encompasses vs your social life vs you work life vs your free time vs your family. You can not ever win.

Now let's remove all the friends from the tables and add in topics you love, let's say on Monday you get to sit and talk at the family table. Those friends know on Monday you can not wait to see them. On Tuesday you spend Taco Tuesday with your work life. You even buy taco leggings and live in that moment on Tuesday. Wednesday you are ready to share every tip ever with your mom friends over coffee. You make it indulgent and talk everything mom stuff on Wednesday and it gets you through the week. Thursday you share great recipes with your foodie crowd and review local restaurants. Friday you plan an event. Saturday you clear your pores. Sunday you rest like it is your job. In this setting you are not needing to be everywhere at all times because you have a rhythm to how you see people and both look forward to it. That is the real way to win at your social media.

The key to creating less chaos is to simplify what is making you stressed and create buckets or space for you to bounce around when you need to. You should never have to pick between a real life and a life online. You should never need to be one channel of advertising 24/7 to get sales or grow your business. We are in a world where people cancel overwhelming cable television to limit commercials and focus on channels that they care about. People don't want to show up to a social gathering on the internet just to be sold to after canceling one of the largest advertising outlets, media.

What they do want is to feel empowered, encouraged, educated, and energized. They need less pain and stress, more fun and good feelings. You have the opportunity to be that answer within your branding. That is not saying that ever post needs you to be positive, if you have something that is bad or ugly to talk about…is it also empowering them to take charge? If you have something negative and painful, are you also telling them how they can help? If you have something strong and hard to discuss, are you helping them have an outlet? You can be yourself and still offer a way to gain back control. It causes people to be inspired instead of broken down. No one wants to have a rough day and then feel broken down online also.

When it comes to social media, people can either go towards the light and love or dark and evil(occasionally dark and love), depending on the topics in your bubbles and the branding make whatever you bring up make sense in the big perspective. You can do that with great content and balancing sales/marketing in high-level ways. You can have your cat videos and your political discussions because you know WHY you are talking about it and HOW to bring it up. You have already done two of the scariest things in business: you have answered who your customers are and who your brand is, it is time to kick social media in the rear.

Have you ever moved into an apartment that is fresh carpet, a brand new kitchen, and a gorgeous new paint job? (I am not saying glamorous, I'm saying new.) Ok so imagine you are just as 'fresh' on how to clean a house or make a life. You are going to make a mess, probably not clean enough, buy 8 ketchups because of disorganization, and not have the best design skills(picture inflatable couches and bed sheets over curtain rods.) This is your social media right now. You ran into this new fun place, you made a giant mess in cat videos, glitter nails, and memes. You got drunk and posted crazy bad pictures in 2009. You got into highly political and not on brand conversations. You went live and stared at the camera like a baby owl. It is exciting and fun. Again, Yayyy.

Grab a broom, it is time to open the windows and clean this place up. Your mother is coming and she is bringing her judgey friends.

I am going to now paint two pictures of life:

**Old way:** Let me slap this logo on every single quote, flower, or photo. Then spam the heck out of people until they see us, then pray they hear our message while we yell it and squirt face cream at them. We went live and possibly cursed while failing to put on makeup well and suggested we knew what we were doing. We private messaged people with horrible illnesses suggesting we have a cure all. We randomly post stuff that come across our feed that is divisive, vulgar, or weird and get caught up in topics that don't connect people. We also make sure all our friends know they are fat, ugly, stupid, or sick and ARE REQUIRED TO BUY OUR PRODUCT TO FIX THEIR FACE/BUTT/LIFE. We claim to be niche but barely understand what that means. We failed to read the room on a day of national tragedy or we posted fake news. We then add in a sales graphic or a coupon after starting a fight between all of our relatives over grandma's recipes. While they were yelling at their screen they couldn't even see our face because our profile is a GIANT logo for weight loss. Cool. If you have never seen a logo across a dog's face or child's butt, be thankful. Yayyyyy-yyy. NO.

**DO NOT FEEL AWKWARD, WE HAVE ALL DONE THIS.** I made this list from friends telling me their worst offenses, even adding in my own! We all learn together, right! We all know junk food is bad, we all still catch ourselves spoon deep in a container of pb candies in popcorn on a bad day. It is ok!

**New way: we are about to break a few rules and a few boundaries.**

*Content over confusion*

Last chapter, we made this amazing bubble chart! It has your social circles, which also connect to your interests, hobbies, and connections. This bubble chart also gives you topics and people! You know who you want to talk to about what you love(and discovered in the other chapters), now you need to decide HOW and WHERE you want them to hear your voice.

"Content" can be confusing based on how deep you get on a google search. I just did one, I can either talk to you about 101 ways to build content, 75 types of content to drive traffic to your website, or 7 main types of content that will fill your marketing calendar. Clap, clap, clap. Wake up! Did I lose you? I genuinely believe that people make things harder than they need to be so that people overwhelm them self. Here, let me hand you 80 pounds of crap to read while you don't realize I am attempting to use my own advice to drive traffic by using 80 key words. Now did I really lose you? Come back to me!

Ok so, the real info you need to understand is the word 'content' seems to change based on the community. Content is the meat and potatoes that fits inside the side dishes of memes, cat videos, and fun quotes; unless that is your brand and then it becomes content. It's confusing. Let's create a bucket system so you know what you are doing.

**There are four outcomes to strongly consider when we talk content marketing:**

-**To entertain** – this will have a strong emotional appeal to an audience, making it very shareable.

Sasha's Translation: Make them laugh or cry, make them react.

Example:Cat videos, quotes, memes. People love social because they want to be happy, be loved, be admired, be sad, connect with others, and have fun. Be the fun.

-**To educate** – this will allow for a wide reach especially for those who might not be in the know about products or services just yet.

Again, this is often very shareable.

Sasha's Translation: Make them feel smart

Example:Make the familiar strange like new recipes, or the strange familiar like a new type of skincare steps with the same favorite products. Some companies don't need just to build brand awareness; they need to build awareness of whole product categories. Teach them about how you create products, the special process, or the bold ingredient already in it that is now trending.

**-To persuade** – This is slightly more emotionally charged; content that gradually changes the mind of the consumer (I say consumer as persuasive content will often be used in a product sense).

Sasha's Translation: Make the world make more sense

Example: Your audience is more likely to be persuaded by your content if they find you credible and trustworthy. To add credibility to your brand, start by identifying influential content contributors from within your industry. Read publications, competitor blogs, social posts, and more in-depth content like ebooks to find creators that match both your brand and marketing needs. Link to trusted third-party sources to validate your content. Use examples or quotes from respected influencers. Highlight your company history, expertise, or awards. Encourage and share customer testimonials and product reviews.

-**To convert** – Content that is more often than

not rational than emotional as you will need a decision-making brain when considering what a conversion piece has to offer you.

Sasha's Translation: Make your products or service the answer

Example: When it comes to converting customers, the secret is simple: understand what the buyer desperately wants and how they want it. Most want it fast and convenient. Your headline or title is the first thing the audience notices about your content. Whether or not the headline captivates them will likely determine if they continue reading, watch, or listen to the content, or bounce. In other words, your headline or title is the bait, and your caption, intro, or description is the hook. Intro or description needs to be to the point and should clearly explain how customers can benefit from the media. Don't forget to add visuals. If you're quoting studies or stats to support your point, include charts and graphs or infographics for further validity. Make everything accessible and easy to read. You want to be clear in your message, relevant to the info your customers are normally getting. Help them make a clear decisions, fast.

**The next turn of scary is Marketing Content vs Sales Content:**

**Marketing content** builds authority, generates leads and establishes an unmistakable identity for the company within its market.

Sasha's Translation: You are an expert, teach

them.

Example: I think Educational and Persuasive answers to this bucket.

**Sales content** exists to communicate urgency, prove the value of a solution.

Sasha's Translation: You are a sales person, sell them something that fixes a need.

Example: I feel Entertaining and Converting answers to this bucket.

**The types of info to fill these buckets:**

-Video: Youtube, Snapchat, Facebook stories, IG stories and TV, and TikTok/Musically

-Pictures: IG profiles, Facebook profiles, Flikr

-Words: blog posting and articles

## This Doesn't Make Me An Expert

*Now that you basically have a degree*

Now that we technically only need two buckets with a couple of subsections, we can start talking about this knowledge in a fundamental way so that you do not feel like you are needing to do everything all over at the same time.

This is a great time to PAUSE, and go back to the question: who do you want to talk to, and where do you need to speak to them so they hear you?

### START WITH THE TOPICS FROM YOUR BUBBLES

Now that we have clarified your branding, we want to also clarify the interests and topics that connect you to your people. If you stray from those after starting a business, people will think you turned into a stereotype. We do not want you to EVER become just a logo and a graphic or corporate ad. You are the thing that needs to be the foundation of your interactions on social media. Anyone can go follow the corporate sites for a brand or business, people want to trust and talk to people about what to buy, that is why influencers do not have a logo posted across their faces.

So what did you do before you joined (insert company) or started (insert traditional business)? Did you have a life, hobbies, habits? Did you run everyday with a running club? Paint pottery at the YMCA? Go to every playdate with the moms on your military base? Have people over for coffee or dinner? You are about to start doing ALL of that again. The second you stopped being yourself, your circle noticed and that causes people to believe you are now a robot spitting out one-liners about your business.

The best way to move forward is to go back to who you were! Call up the friends, get those yoga pants out, and DIVE in with a full calendar. Online you are going to make the drastic steps and remove anything that is not personal. If you didn't take the pic, your people might not want to see it! They want to see your products how you use them, not in a generic way. If you don't have one on hand to use it, post a pic about an orange and talk about citrus. If you can't do that, talk about the reason you love the purpose of your business. Maybe you take your team to volunteer at a food kitchen and post a recipe. Or you go to an event and take a pic of the coffee that kept you up after a late night of brainstorming. Talk about your life not just your business. PEOPLE WANT YOU TO BE REAL. This is how the people will trust that you aren't just selling them on something that is hard to picture in their life. They want to see how it is part of yours. The bubbles become more and more important then in creating actual content vs just posting advertising until they all unfriend. The interests become your topics that combine your friend groups. The people are the audience that want to hear more about the topic that connects you. As you get really great at this, people and interests will start to blend and overlap because you become the thing they have in common. A great example of this can be the moment you find a friend from PTA also going to your grocery store. You are connected not only by the kids school PTA but now because you shop in the same area of town. Another example can be church friends showing up for a networking meeting for your company. You can start to combine talking about church events with talking about networking events.

Ok, now we are going to do that for all your media: we are going to go find you people that want to talk to you about cool stuff you love, with people that also want to talk to you about different stuff you love…but without either feeling like you have started to be a spam machine monster from the depths of Direct Sales or Entrepreneur hell. ACTUAL YAY!

**You also have a few ways to use topics to connect:**

-Short: hashtags and keywords

-Medium: Captions, Descriptions, and status

-Long: articles, listicles, and blog posting

Use the topics to figure out what you post. If your topic is food, use food as a hashtag to find others. Use food as the theme to your picture captions. Use food as a category on your blog.

ONCE YOUR KNOW YOUR TOPICS, DELETE ANYTHING THAT DOES NOT SPEAK ABOUT THOSE TOPICS. IT IS IRRELEVANT.

WHERE AND WHAT PLATFORMS DO "YOUR PEOPLE" HANG OUT? GO THERE FIRST.

### Social networking sites

Most of us are familiar with social networking sites like Facebook, Twitter, and LinkedIn.

These platforms help us connect with friends, family, and brands. They encourage knowledge-sharing and are all about personal, human-to-human interaction.

HOW DO I USE THESE: Create ads depending on the rules in your policies and procedures, network with customers and teammates, use hashtags to find people interested in your same topics.

**Social review sites**

Review sites like Yelp, Sephora, Ulta, Influenster, and TripAdvisor display reviews from community members for all sorts of locations and experiences. This eliminates a lot of the guesswork that goes into trying a restaurant, buying a product, or booking a hotel. Not sure it's the right thing for you? Check out the reviews and you'll know.

HOW DO I USE THESE: Understand the customers perspective on products on the market and learn how to solve issues by watching other companies interact with their customers. I like to be on sites that review topics I have in my bubbles so I am part of that conversation.

**Image sharing sites**

Visual content like images, infographics, and illustrations capture our hearts, eyes and imaginations. Social media platforms like Instagram, Imgur, and Snapchat are designed to amplify the power of image sharing.

Users create and share unique images that spark conversation and speak for themselves. A picture can be worth a thousand words to your business.

HOW DO I USE THESE: You can run campaigns encouraging users to snap and share a pic with your product and a unique hashtag. By creating and sharing your own images, you can also inspire and engage your audience to bond over a shared interest.

**Video hosting sites**

YouTube revolutionized the way we watch, create, and think about video. It transformed the medium into something accessible. Video hosting platforms like YouTube, Periscope, Tiktok, and Vimeo help creators put together content and share it to a platform optimized for streaming. This accessibility makes video a super important medium.

HOW DO I USE THESE: Create quality content and connect with community and comment sections about your topics.

## Community blogs

Sometimes an image or post isn't complex enough for the message you've got to share, but not everyone on the internet wants to run a blog from a self-hosted website. That's a lot of work.

Shared blogging platforms like Medium and Tumblr give people a space to express their thoughts and help connect them with readers.

If you do want to set up a full blog you can look up Weebly, Wix, and Wordpress tutorials.

HOW DO I USE THESE: Test the waters before diving into a major Wordpress website and create a community following around your topics, products, and services. You can start creating educational, persuasive, and entertaining content on these sites. Then you can feed that content to others platforms. If you do have a hosted website, you can also use community blogging platforms to share, re-purpose, and re-post older content and expose it to a new audience.

**Discussion sites**

While most of us have seen many a heated discussion happen on Facebook, discussion sites like Reddit and Quora are specifically designed to spark a conversation. Anyone is free to ask a question or make a statement, and this attracts people with shared interests and curiosities. However, unlike Facebook and Instagram, users tend to give out less identifiable information.

HOW DO I USE THESE: With a bit of research, you can find and engage people in your field, discover what they're asking, and use this as a starting point for your content marketing strategy. Quora asks questions, by answering them can help establish you as a thought leader and drive more traffic to your site.

**Sharing economy networks**

Sites like Uber, AirBandB, Lyft, and Rover aren't just a cool place to find cheap hotel rentals, get a ride, or a pet sitter. Sharing economy networks bring people who've got something they want to share together with the people who need it. You can find many pulling side hustles and in industries that connect with yours. These communities provide opportunities that won't exist otherwise by pooling resources on a large scale that wouldn't be possible without tech.

This Doesn't Make Me An Expert

HOW DO I USE THESE: Depending on the site you chose to interact with, you can start connecting and networking for office space, services, and products that help you all win.

### USING YOUR BRANDING AND BUSINESS TITLE, SECURE YOUR INFO ON ALL PLATFORMS.

Set the tone by setting up all profiles effectively so they know it is you. Then on EVERY platform, you are going to have the same profile pic of YOUR FACE. You will then add in the same links and start with a similar description. If you are a person from 0-30 I (joking) will allow a max of 3 emoji, zero with tongues out. And please do not include a profile pic of your dog, unless it is literally your dog's profile.

Why is this important? Other than sounding

silly and bossy, there is a reason people connect better with professionals with their faces in their profile. Even babies want to see your face to know if they can trust you. Since we are currently in the business of building trust and connection, give it a go. Does the picture have to be absolutely perfect and professionally done? NO. I would love it if the world could afford headshots, but be realistic. Many are photoshopped and you want people to be able to recognize you like the famous person you will eventually be. Mine were done at an event for Smashbox Cosmetics by a great photog, but you can have your husband take a pic in front of a white sheet. The bigger point is that it is your face, the smaller focus is perfection and fakeness. I guarantee you are a beautiful creature we all will love to see. Do it.

Examples: Go find PoshSwederSide or SashaSweder on almost every type of social and you will find my face.

You can even email me at one of the usernames also.

You will also see almost consistent descriptions and profile pics. I am sure there is some account somewhere I forgot and you will have fun finding!

GET TO KNOW YOUR AUDIENCE. MAKE SURE THEY GET TO KNOW YOU ALSO.

Connect the dots on your IAM bubble by blogging so it pushes info to your social and email list.

Many have vulnerable spots in our past history because life is not black and white, there is often grey. I say this because many will look at some of their bubbles and see topics that they do not want to discuss out loud, never mind making a post online. Sorry but not sorry, I guarantee you are not alone in whatever happened. The curse behind this feeling, someone else in your audience has also had whatever it is happen and could really use someone not being sugar coated about it. The good news is courage can be typing the words and hitting post. While not every crazy tale should be told in documented proof, many need to feel more connected in this digital age and this is one way you can help your audience understand who you are and why they should trust you.

The part that makes this scary is when you are an "oversharer" because you do not know your audience well enough to blurt out your story. You need to know who you are talking to and where to say it, once again returning to the entire point of our chapter!

Let's start by understanding the basics. In your bubbles you will have people also listed, spouse or SO, kids, animals, friends, and people that you spend a lot of time with and the areas of interest that they connect you to. Remember, without the bubble of the handsome husband I wouldn't connect to the military community as much. Therefore when I speak about the hard life of him deploying I speak to that topic honestly and authentically. If I started some post about being a service member and not had been one, that would be inauthentic unless I was going off of his experiences and used his story. If I then wanted to be even more specific I could talk about life as an Air Force wife but couldn't speak as authentically about the life of a Navy wife without making assumptions. I also would need to talk to an actual Firefighter wife before assuming their paths had any similarity to a military wife path because I have zero experience with those challenges. All of these examples wrap up to how topics can each be very personal and require honest perspectives.

If you have a hobby on there that you know only some about you can speak honestly by telling your audience you are learning. The expectation that you are immediately a world class chef will go away if you join a cooking business when you tell them that you are just learning and then they want to cheer for you as you burn food. Being vulnerable about learning can also be tough, but it is something that people like to connect about and share tips. It can be a great way to bond. Personally, I am making a big point about my lack of hair-styling experience because I figure eventually some one will sit and show me how to make my hair curl perfectly. It follows the theory that if you ask enough or look like a hot mess enough people will help or they will high five you when you hit your goal. They tend to judge less when they get to know your struggles, in my case burns and bruising.

Another way to be vulnerable with your audience is being upfront about mistakes and hardships. If you forgot to post, be honest. If you have a bad day, I bet they have had one too. If you go through mental health issues and want to show them why you are so damn cheery all the time, say it. Not everyone wants to deal with depression by seeing more sadness. I surf memes and funny stuff when I feel the worst and share it then also. That doesn't mean I am always butterflies and sunshine, it means I needed this sunshine also. I have canceled events I had scheduled. I have forgotten to mail giveaways. Be a human. It is ok to be a human. One more time for the people in the back: BE. A. HUMAN.

After you are done with identifying topics, creating content, and using your bubbles to find your audience, make sure all your info on social is linked up the right way so that you get the most power to your post which requires a process for how to market your content.

**We start by creating a marketing strategy for your content:**

-You plan: You come up with an idea to talk about

-You create: Ebook, Podcast, E-Course, Presentation, Photo, Press-Release, Webinar, Kits, Videos and a Blog Post about that topic

-You publish: You publish the info online through your website, youtube channel, or emails.

-You promote: You then put the info on your social media platforms linking back to the original published info.

-You manage and analyze the data from insights and sales.

## TOOLS AND RESOURCES HOW TO LEARN WAY MORE

Check out the last few chapters for books and social links how to help you stand out.

### SOCIAL MEDIA CHALLENGE

1. IDENTIFY YOUR TOPICS
2. IDENTIFY YOUR AUDIENCE
3. IDENTIFY YOUR TYPES OF CONTENT
4. IDENTIFY AND SET UP YOUR SOCIAL PROFILES
5. CREATE A MARKETING STRATEGY
6. START CREATING AND MARKETING SO YOU CAN ANALYZE DATA
7. RESPOND TO DATA BY CREATING MORE OF WHAT IS SUCCEEDING
8. REPOST SUCCESSFUL INFO USING POST SCHEDULING TO MAXIMIZE POWER IN CONTENT CREATED.

# CHAPTER 7
# NO, SHE WASN'T.
## No, she wasn't throwing parties.

And now we are going to get into a similar conversation but on a much more silly topic: parties, events, and get togethers. We are going to start small and build up to vendor event experiences in the next chapter. For many years, many have ignored the connection between branding and building an event strategy. I also completely ignored that I had experience with events even when walking into vendor events. If you are in Direct Sales, parties can be a bad word. In traditional storefronts, it is a foreign language I had never learned. I still can barely wrap my brain them to be honest without thinking about what you are about to learn so

I will be discussing most of this chapter from the perspective of a hospitality management graduate not a direct sales person: catering, weddings, and event management, oh my. Get very excited!

*The 5 Ws and How*

In all situations you will need to answer this same round of questions when planning your next steps:

- Who are your guests? How many people?
- What is your event?
- When is your event?
- Where is your event?
- Why is this event happening?
- How much money is in your budget?

*Being Realistic About The Guest List*

Many will make a giant guest list for an event

and assume that when people do not respond to an RSVP or cancel at the last minute is a failure so let's clear that out IMMEDIATELY. 25% of invites sent out in anyway will be ignored and not even seen. In my experience 1/2 that respond will either say they will go or hit maybe on an RSVP and not go or forget. Then out of the rsvp that said yes, only expect people that are ACTIVELY posting in events or taking to your about the event to come. Possibly one or two extra that will not respond and will show up if they are close to you. Every leaders has had a party where no one showed up. Most have parties with between 4-10 people. Larger events will happen maybe once a year or at catalog launches. Personally, my first attempt at a party had two people show up. My second had 4 and I was CONFIDENT is had already won at life. You are still awesome even if people cancel on you. Keep going.

In a vendor event setting, this is a question you will be asking the coordinator before you hand over money. You want to know if this event was held and how many people attended before. You want to know common foot traffic and how to plan for the amount of people in attendance.

*Tone and Theme of The Event*

Based on the people attending and the time of year, you can start to create the tone and theme of the event. For instance, a wedding in the spring will be different than a wedding in the fall. The same goes for your events for your business. If you have a traditional store front you can throw a party in the Spring and create excitement with another theme focus in the Fall, both focused on rewarding your loyal customers and get a lot of amazing traffic inside of your location! If you are in direct sales, you can prepare a theme party schedule for loyal customers based on monthly themes and different collections or focuses in your product line.

In a vendor event setting, this is also relevant for the set up you plan out! You would not make the same set up at a wedding event as a baby event or home show. Knowing and using the theme to connect with the guests will be important to show you know your audience while you are there.

*Site, Setting, Scene*

Where is your event being held is important

in a traditional and direct sales sense. I have seen skincare parties for 10 people and 1 bathroom sink. I have also seen businesses hold vendor festivals and not have operational bathrooms. These are both HORRIBLE ideas, which makes the setting and location very important as you plan your event.

If you are holding your event offline, make sure you visit the location in advance to collect important info. As you hold more events in multiple locations will learn how to gather a kit of essentials like sharpies, tape, pens, paper, and other items important for your style of business. This way you can set up nearly anywhere and get comfy.

If you are holding events online you can use this moment to also consider the location of the event like groups vs events vs chats vs live. You can create your own setting but you need to understand the platform you are picking to hold the event. Is your internet consistent? Are there limitations you need to plan ahead for and adapt to?

If we are talking about a vendor event, this is also the moment you consider whether or not you need electrical outlets, tables, and curtains or if items are all furnished by your coordinator. In the event planning industry we call this a blank slate or all in, referring to everything be all included.

*Planning Organization is Key*

When most professionals have gathered the basic info, they start a master event book. I would highly suggest the same so that you can learn just as much and start to have a routine! You can keep receipts and contact info in a binder or your can have a folder online perfect for graphics and stuff you reuse for themes and situations.

In this binder or folder we want to include:
- Contact Sheets for the people participating
- Contracts for locations and vendors
- Any correspondence to and from about that event
- Host coaching info for Direct Sales events
- A basic budget for the event
- Receipts for inventory and supplies
- Any insurance info for vender events
- Venue directions and floor plans
- Transportation and accommodation info
- Guest list and responses

- Timeline plans for when you do what, great also for online events
- Notes
- Miscellaneous info

*Creating a Timeline*

In the next few sections I have drilled down on tasks you may be completing around certain times before, during, and after an online party, an in person party, and a vendor event. There are also info on what a traditional event timeline looks like. They are all very similar and we can all learn from each other.

Notice along the way the moments you are focused on building entertainment, education, persuading moments, and converting info. That knowledge is about to change your entire life. Let's have fun!

*6 months or more in advance*

Vendor Events can be booked very far out, some get a discount on booking at the event the year before. If you can do it, planning ahead can be a great benefit as long as the coordinator is trust worthy and not at risk. Make sure the refund policy is something you accept.

If you are doing a lot of vendor events, prepare a list of customers you meet every year at these events so you can email them to remind them.

If you have not booked an event before you can participate and take notes on whether people are making money. This is especially helpful if you are new to the area or a new business, you can go to local events and check them out and decide which will be best for your brand and your business style. Pay attention to how happy the vendors are, if people are shopping, if the location looks like you need a tent or special equipment, and if it is advertising well within the community.

### Four months or more

If you have been booking vendor events you can reconfirm you have the right amount of inventory on hand and equipment based on the needs of the event coming up. I would confirm all payments and redefine your timeline for your event days leading up. Make sure any save the dates for customers that normally attend are sent out. You can also confirm deposits have been made and no plans have changed from the venue.

This is also a great time to add the vendor

event info to your social platforms and start to promote with your followers.

*Two or three months or before*

Finalize the theme, menu, decor, and details. Make sure you have business cards, merchandise, and paperwork for inside the event. Mail out formal invites. Confirm your placement inside of a convention center or location from the coordinator. Review your booth or party staffing options. If you have a day job, coordinate your time off.

*One month or before*

Consider any food and beverages on site. This can finalize a menu card and meal plan if needed. Confirm all electrical and furnishing needs. Formulate a plan for loading into the event and loading out for a party or a vendor event. Create a show special or a party special that is within budget. Gather any giveaways or auction items. Finalize and print programs and paperwork. Label all products.

*Two weeks before*

If you are working on a traditional event you are confirming details like loading schedules, credentials, and set up. For vendor events you want to know your placement in the room, officially and if you need to know anything for loading in and out.

Many book online parties two weeks out MAXIMUM and begin host coaching at that point. Booking farther out tends to encourage more cancellations since most people don't keep their calendars that far in advance and many things can come up. If you have not already, make sure you schedule a time to discuss detail on the phone by video or call. You want to get to know them and why they want to hold the event. Many also give hosts a packet of basic info. Some things you could include in your packet: catalogs, order forms, the current host special and a letter thanking them for hosting and giving them a bit of what is to come. Scheduling 2 weeks ahead will give you and your host plenty of time to create a guest list, get invitations sent out and (hopefully) get another booking or two from your host's friends. Remember, be realistic and OVER INVITE but stay under 50 names. Make sure your host can PERSONALLY reach out to ever person on the list. Set the time line and info from before with the host so that they can start to talk to guests about the event coming up. Start a notebook, binder, or folder similar to the event book and coordinate details. Set up the group/event/or platform you will be holding the event on and any info you need to set up on your website. Some like groups and some like events, it all depends on the limitation and advantages currently available, go with your gut and Google. Set up public events also on your social media so that people can see the event and help your host out if they are shopping, many also do this so that they can show off that their calendar is full. You can also boost an event by paying causing more attention also, but this is depending on your company's policies. A great tip I have heard is also to have the party inside of a group so that if the person decides to join after the party, they already have a list of customers started. This is also a great moment for you to send out invites off line also.

If your product or service is something you can sample and share this is a great moment for them to create a wishlist and to get samples in the hands of the host so they can start inviting people as they try and love the products. Many do giveaways and challenges based on sharing the products in the events. This is again shadowing back to building trust and persuading with reviews and educating with product info.

Many coach each Host to include three things in their personal party invite, which is typically sent via text or Facebook Messenger: Why they love the product, Why they decided to host, Why they thought to specifically invite that person. Then the host asks if their friend would like an invitation to the party.

After the guest says YES (or maybe), the host can reply back with the group link and say, "Click here to request to join the party." That way the host does not add anyone who hasn't asked to attend the party.

Set alarms in your phone to either contact your host 3 times before the party or to follow up with your event coordinator. The three times are: 1 week, 3 days, day before. I also suggest adding their phone numbers into your phone for the day of.

### One week before

Follow-up with your host one week after the booking to be sure they have everything they need and to answer any questions they may have. This is a great time to plan ahead for guests that are local and cancel so they can 'party from home'. It sometimes takes a bit of coaxing to help a host understand that multiple invitations to each guest is not "bothering" people, it's making sure that busy people know they are invited because not everyone pays attention to the same channels.

In a traditional store front situation, you can set up an online discount sale only for loyalty program users or a coupon code that gets them a free treat when they can make it in. This is a great time to reach out to local customers and also remind anyone near your vendor location of the event in a week and a deal if they show up.

This is also a great time to follow up on missing packages. Confirm times everyone is arriving for in person parties or vendor events. Prepare balance payments for anything not paid for yet. Adjust anything needed based on the formal guest lists.

### Three days before the event

Call, text, or video chat your host one to two days before the party to re-confirm and cover any last minute details. Ask if they have gotten any outside orders, and how many guests are planning to be there. Encourage them to confirm all RSVPs are still accurate to make sure no one had plans change.

### Day before the event

Check I with all staff expected the vendor events or party. Confirm time for set up for parties, start setting up the vendor booth. Pack up your car with stuff if you have an in person party or a local small event. Use your checklists and info in your binder to confirm you have all the items needed to be able to set up. Plan your outfit out and wash anything needed so that you look your best. You don't have to look fancy, you need to look consistent with your branding.

### Day of the event

Confirm everyone is there to set up on time, and have it all set up 10 mins before guests start arriving. You want to have time to talk to the host and get to know the guests before you start selling.

Make sure you eat way before a party or vendor event and have plans for breaks if the event is longer than 2 hours. You will need to go to the bathroom, know where it is.

## This Doesn't Make Me An Expert

On the night of the party, recognize your host and publicly thank them for inviting you into their home. Give them a free hostess gift just for holding the party, and offer a free gift right then to anyone who books a party off theirs.

Here are two examples of common online parties, one focused on products and the other on growing a team.

*A common direct sales facebook party framework*
1. Welcome Post and Introduce Yourself
2. Introduce Your Company
3. What helps your company stand apart
4. Tell them what time and what day you are going live to discuss the special and the products
5. A warning post 15 mins before you go live
6. Remind them of any deals that help them save, be clear and concise
7. Tell them about the advantages to hosting
8. Then the advantages to joining your company or joining your loyalty program
9. Thank them from coming

10. Thank your host

## A common direct sales facebook opportunity event framework

1. Welcome Post and Introduce Yourself
2. Introduce Your Company
3. What helps your company stand apart
4. Then the advantages to joining your company or joining your loyalty program
5. How do they get paid?
6. What kind of training?
7. Where do they go for support?
8. Are there other fun advantages to being with your company?
9. How do they sign up?
10. Thank them for coming.

## After the event

Collect all the outside orders your hostess collected and finalize her party as quickly as possible. After all money is collected, be sure they order arrives on time and intact. Communicate with them often to deal with any issues that may arrive such as damaged products or delayed shipments.

A day or two after the party, call your host

and thank her again for all she did. Send her a postcard or note card in the mail to say thank you more formally. Send a thank you to the vendors near you at the vendor event or to anyone that participated in your traditional event. You could include a business card magnet so they can call you if they have questions, needs anything, or for when they are ready to rebook.

Call your host after all orders have been delivered to be sure them and their guests were pleased with their products. Ask them if they knows anyone else who may want to book a party or join your team. Encourage them to call you if they have any questions at any time.

Set an alert in your calendar to either connect with your host in 4-6 months, or the event coordinator.

*Four to Six Month Later*

Call your host again about four to six months after their party and invite them to book another. Tell them about any new host products or incentives you have to offer and give them an added discount such as 10% off any one item for being a repeat host.

## I COULD ISSUE YOU A CHALLENGE BUT I AM BETTING YOU EITHER NEED A NAP OR

This Doesn't Make Me An Expert

# YOUR MIND IS RACING. GO TAKE OVER THE WORLD.

## CHAPTER 8
## NO, SHE ISN'T.
### No, she isn't a good leader and can't learn.

........................................................

Ok so here we are at the last real instructional chapter and we have been through SO MUCH together. You have launched yourself, you have built a brand, you have a social media strategy that would make an IT guy proud, you understand how to intertwine different times of events, and now you have done the impossible: you either hired a person or you had a brave soul join your team.

Let's take a breath and enjoy this moment, you are by title a leader. This is exciting and thrilling and terrifying. If you paused at the way I said that first sentence you have great reason, many that have not listened to hours of leadership videos on social media believe that the second you are handed a title, you are the leader. It is a common trap in management that takes understanding and patience to completely connect with. Let's dive in.

I am a strong subscriber to thinking of customers, teammates, new hires, and people around you as relationships. In relationships, you can have difficult dynamics that are seen and unseen. You have outside factors influencing the connection and contraction. You also have experiences in life that can change both people in the relationship, you either need to adapt or depart. So with all of that in a relationship, it is very difficult to see leadership as a simple step by step process to being awesome.

There is no direct path because you are not just working on tasks but also bonding or NOT bonding. So when it comes down to leading, I see it not as a bunch of levels and not really as languages of affection. I see it more as a real relationship, and hopefully no one will find themselves yelling in the break room.

*That first date*

This is both the best of it but can be scary. You know nothing about each other and you go on a date. You need to ask great questions to see what you have in common. In leadership you may have just hired this person or they may have just joined your team. Sometimes people that were super familiar outside of your business may come in and have assumptions on your business that will need to be handled. You also need to set good expectations just like you would to a new hire and make sure they are receiving quality training. Give them your time, but make sure they are using it wisely so they can build up strength.

### YOU ARE DATING

You are showing up cute to work, you flirt with new projects, you are trying your hardest to make compromises and find things that are fun to do. This is the person that joined your team and got started strong, they know what they are doing and able to be more independent. You still spend lots of time on fundamentals but you do not need to hand hold as much to be seen together. This is a great time to shout out all the great things they are accomplishing and build trust that you will be there when they hit a road block.

For a traditional store front, you have given them on boarding training and started to help them make decisions on their own that fall within the job description. You are not adding on too many projects but you are seeing if they can coast without constant guidance.

They see you as a leader but they have not fully gotten to know you yet and you may have not even had differences yet. Everybody is settling into their roles.

### YOU ARE ENGAGED

You have made that commitment and decided to dive in to your second or third job in this business. You have also started taking some of the traits you saw as cute seriously and read the entire health benefits option or you are building a team with over 10 frontline. Since the roles are starting to get more serious and you have delegated more responsibility you may start assessing their productivity and they may start assessing if they like your leadership style. It is normal for some fighting because both are starting to consider their roles more seriously in the big picture. They may ask for more training, more work, and more space. All perfectly natural. When you give it, it can help build trust and understanding. When they see results from what you are teaching them and listening to requests then they start to see you as someone they may like to follow and learn from.

### YOU ARE MARRIED

This is when we start talking about a traditional business lasting more than 5-10 years and has finally hit the red. This is a strong and stable start to a long term plan of building your teams. Some know this the second they join, some need years to get here. You may quit your side jobs and focus on a single business at this point or you may sign serious leases. Be careful and don't get so comfortable that you lose yourself into the mix. Make sure you are making decisions that are financial on facts not feelings so that debt doesn't crush you because opening a bakery or stating a business can cost you a lot.

This is a serious partnership on the field, start to handle it that way. You will NOT always agree. You will NOT always have the same goals but you get your hands dirty and get to real work. This is when a leader is also getting great at leading themselves and their own teams.

## YOU ARE DIVORCING or BREAK UPS

This one I only have experience about from the outside so it can be difficult but I have had friendships rapidly implode so I am going to go with that experience. People are going to leave. You do not want to hold people hostage to your business or your team page just like in life. I have had teammates leave after learning all they could and turning that knowledge into profitable business and others leave angry because you couldn't work their business for them. Either way, you will be ok. You either grow to learn how to fix the mistakes or learn to accept things you had no control over or be proud of them for moving on so wonderfully.

Occasionally, teammates may start to develop a leadership style that is opposite or similar to yours. Some will look to emulate people that are mentors and some will start to reject styles around them so that they can cause their groups to solidify. I always think of it as moms and kids, if you are like your mom or you are like your grandma and you mom is an absolute rebel. Patterns of rebellion in leadership chains. You love the leader farther away because the are not actually your direct and you push away your direct because they are closer. If they mimic your style they may not feel confident yet and will form their own style in time. If they rebel, it is not personal even when it feels like it.

The worst that can happen is lingering, when

the relationship is over or the situation is solved and it is time for separation. Just like it not healthy for the family to have the parents fighting ugly, it is not any better for leadership or your team to be in a toxic work place. When, how, and what happens next in that situation is up to you, your leadership, and your company. In the real world, it is all up to your labor laws and if your team needs a different leader or you need a different team. Hard choices will happen, people will be hurt. Focus on the bigger picture not the short term. You will be ok. It will be ok.

That analogy actually holds up pretty well! Interesting! While it definitely does not cover everything when it comes to leadership, I could literally write an entire book just about styles, types of motivation, and systems. I'll do that later this year. But for now, start to look at how you are leading in your life, many do not notice what they are capable of and many do not see those that they work with as relationships. When you see that people will always be flawed, plan for ways to support them the best you can with all you can. If they love it, great. If they don't, you tried your best.

You can learn how to be anything, including a great leader. You just need to open your heart and reach out for resources. You can learn to listen better, try harder, and think slower. You can do this.

## CHAPTER 9

## I CAN, I WILL, I JUST DID.

I Can Be Everything I Was Not Yesterday.
I Will Grow Stronger Every Year.
I Did Give This My All Even When Tired.
Here Are All Of The Lessons I Learned Along The Way:

1. If you can dream it, you can do it.

While David was gone I did one of those silly Pinterest crafts where you pick a quote and put stickers on a canvas and paint over the stickers. Then you peel off the stickers. This quote was the one I would stare at for hours when I had no clue what to do next. I painted it rainbow colors like pixie dust and magic, it would cause me to remember that Disney World contained so much more in ideas than anyone had ever seen before and many didn't believe in that dream.

No one needs to believe in what you are doing except for you. Go pick yourself a quote and put it on your wall, fridge, or mirror. Right now.

A lot of my quotes come from music or movies because for about 20 years I hated reading. You can follow me and my playlists on YouTube and Apple Music:

-https://www.Youtube.com/c/sashasweder-posh

-https://itunes.apple.com/us/playlist/66daysofposh/pl.u-V9D7vddSBv9gD05

2. Just because you do not know how to do something does not mean you can not learn how. There are free or close to free resources everywhere. On my most frugal days I will bring a mug of coffee and stand in the business section in the local library. Mine has a magical

view of my Pikes Peak, figure out your most favorite spot in your most favorite local library and MOVE in. You are not alone, someone has tried to figure out whatever you are struggling with and can teach you how to tackle your biggest roadblocks. Newsflash also, you can take a book off the shelf at chain or local bookstore, walk into the cafe and get glass of free water and sit there from open to close learning. Martin Luther King Jr told us, "If you can't fly, then run. if you can't run, then walk. If you can't walk, then crawl, but by all means, keep moving." If you can not get to the library search the internet for free copies. If you can't stack up books, get an Amazon Kindle account. If you can not sit and read, you get an audiobook version. If you can not read well, watch a video on youtube. If you can not watch a video, take a local class. DO NOT LOOK AT YOUR ROADBLOCKS AND ACCEPT THEM. Do the best you can, with what you have until you have more and can reassess.

3. Ask for help until you get it. My son has social issues that will not only cause him to need help, but will prevent him from verbalizing that need for help. He had a long list of reasons he was scared to ask for help. The scariest moment for me in Florida was him swimming in a pool and nearly drowning because he couldn't and wouldn't yell out. He is a smaller child and thought the kids would think he was weak. He was new and didn't know who to ask. He was worried he would never get to go to a birthday party again. He didn't want to leave the pool. All of these reasons could have cost him his

life. Stubbornness is the trait that this normally shows up as in others, so many misunderstand him. We learned that the best way to manage this was two options, teach him to swim and teach him how to ask for help even if it is uncomfortable. If you do not reach out, you can drown. People want to help each other, people have experience and can help. YOU HAVE TO ASK. If the first person doesn't help you keep going. You keep asking. You find the right one to stop and help. If you give up because one person will not help you succeed, you give up on your future self. In your heart, I am confident, you know that no one wants you to fail. No one wants you to give up. Someone will always help. Customers, leaders, fellow business owners, fellow vendors, teammates, people walking down the street, just ASK.

4. Know yourself and balance your weaknesses. This one is very hard because many of us have negative self-talk so this can get grey. There is a large difference is a weakness from not even try to be good at it and a weakness you haven't tried out yet. Like I have said and will say in this list, LEARN. But there will be some situations and weaknesses you cannot teach yourself out of. Accept them and find a balance. If you suck at money, get a great accountant you can trust that is vetted. If you can not work social media, hire a trustworthy and strong teen that will run it confidently with your brand in mind. If you suck at team building, find a person that doesn't and teach them sales. If you suck at sales, find a person that doesn't and teach them how to team build. Use your

frontline as a gas pedal and brake for your business and team. Need more energy, add teammates because no one is more excited than a teammate in their 1st 90 days. Need more time to focus on fundamentals, add in friends that are independent. Need more ideas, find people that have been in business. Need more creativity, find people that have never done this before but want to experiment. If you suck at something you have two choices, continue to suck or learn how to get better. I would rather get better and teach someone else how to also suck less tomorrow.

5. Do not be scared to add new people to your circle. I have a lot of fears when it comes to people judging me, I am sure that you know that by chapter 10. New people can be scary when you are overwhelmed and scared to talk

to people. I either have to say NOTHING or EVERYTHING. My mother used to joke that I would meet people and be silent for a while but by the end of the day, you would know everything about me including my Social. Thankful I have learned to stop short of my social, but I come pretty close. Even worse if I have lost all inhibitions when drinking or anxiety really kicks in. Do not worry, if I ever said anything weird to you ever, I like to sort those out while I wash dishes and try to go to sleep. This also includes if I have cut you off while you were talking. I am not always the best at creating clear sentences when my brain starts racing and I have gotten to learn a lot from my son about how this works. This fear has been repeated over and over since deciding to write this book. Anxiety can cause a person to literally freeze in the middle of a sentence. My son used to start editing his words as he spoke and that caused no one to understand his points. My husband often points out that pauses in my thoughts drive him nuts and I OFTEN will start a conversation as if I was speaking to myself for five minutes. I have been called out for my manners and told I was too blunt, even if unintentionally. My favorite is the people that see this as me being rude and abrupt. In reality, I am FREAKING out and trying my hardest to not vomit hoping you will like me and understand me, you may also scare the heck out of me. It gets worse once we have had any tension in conversation ever, I assume you don't understand me. So new people are fun. The best way to beat fear is to do something scary over and over until it is a habit. Go to meetups and be weird. Be your normal self and see who runs and who gets closer. Don't misunderstand, be professional. But do not show up and act like you are the only person fearing judgment. If we didn't all sweat from nerves, no one would have made deodorant. Set up an account on meetup or find a local group on your social. Your first meeting can even be Goat Yoga. I give you permission. Just go meet people. The good ones don't bite as hard.

6. If you hate what you are doing, change how you do it and set a new goal. You do not have to be the same person you were 5 mins ago. Reinvent yourself until the outside matches your inside. Many leaders have joined multiple Direct Sales companies before they had the right fit. Many people in business have

started multiple companies before perfecting their processes. No one expects a person to hit a home run the first time they step up to home plate in Baseball, why would you expect that of yourself. THE DIFFERENCE: gain enough experience that when the right product, service, or situation comes along, do not overwhelm yourself with too many side hustles and undermine your REAL and HONEST opportunity for growth.

7. Build real relationships out of friendship, not just convenience and branding. Not everyone has to be your friend, and not everyone will be NO MATTER WHAT YOU DO FOR THEM, but you have to build relationships that are real or you will always feel insecure in your settings. Friends can be the family you create. And if you

can not find a circle, come sit with us. The only rule, you have to be ready to speak nothing but light and love at all times in this group. We have a group packed with people battling big issues and need that as much as you.

https://www.facebook.com/groups/1112718448785554/

8. You determine how high you fly based on how strong you believe your wings are. IF you wake up every day saying you can't do something, you have 100% chance of not doing something. Self talk is the thing that will crush your dreams. Negativity from inside of you will come out. You will tell yourself to quit everything a thousand times, don't. Be a rebel. Look you in the face and say NOPE. Because the real truth, those are the statements impeded in

your mind that have limited you all your life and just because you quit this, doesn't mean they will go away. Do battle now, while you have the advantage. Prove all of those voices wrong even if it is just that you got out of bed and showered.

9. You can learn to be a good leader if you have your heart in the right place. For every person in the world, there is a different theory about what it takes to be a great leader. Many agree it boils down to two things: the heart to try, and the courage to act. I am happy to fail every day at things as long as I know that I wake up and try again. I am also happy to know that I suck at things when I try new stuff because the courage to act and get in the ring is much more important than standing back waiting to

be perfect. You have to act on instincts so they get stronger. You practice, you get back up, you go to parties that suck, events that are empty, and you try again. You keep going as long as you keep believing you are helping someone else have a better day than the last.

10. Do the things you think you can not do purely for the confidence you get from completing the task not the response. Experiment with life for fun. I attended Cape Cod Sea Camps in Brewster, MA from 6-8 grade. It was the same camp as my grandmother and we had summers that are not easily forgotten. One of the summers I was heading into my Freshman year of High School and we were working as Junior Counselors. A great leader, probably the first encountered had a saying

"Work Hard Play Hard." It really stuck to me and how I pictured my life. (He also had a great affection to Jimmy Buffet music and that helped me when David was at the Citadel. I see you Parrotheads!) We would sit in this cool theater every day for morning announcements and nighttime shows. The banner on the top of the theater said I Can & I Will. All summer we would set goals for awards, trophies, and achievements and it always came back to that saying. I have that on a plaque that is ice blue and silver in my kitchen. Next to that picture, I have a tiny blackboard that says things like "run faster, eat better, try harder, aim higher, love more, day by day, get happier". It reminds me everyday of camp and the things I started the summer thinking I could not do, and the things I had done by the end of that time. It is amazing when you prove yourself and others wrong about your potential. Some where in your heart, you know what you can create. You know your potential to make this path your own, you have the strength to push back.

When I started this book my biggest fear was failing to express and explain to you that you can do what I am doing. There is no special club, no elite credit card, no chosen few. It is hard work and not giving up that got me this far. It took a whole lot of love to build up my company of passionate people, I can not for one second shortchange myself on how impactful my heart was in making that happen. People along the way had to see that I believed in the dream and that I believed in them also. The numbers at that point are silly, the day to day goals are the fluff. It is all about the people. I will never take credit for it all, but I did that. I built that. I joined.

Whatever someone is telling you that you can't do, won't do, shouldn't, do, wouldn't do, didn't do, because it hasn't been done, or isn't getting done; you have to shout it out very clear. I can do this, I will do this. I just did this. Like this:

I told myself I couldn't write a book. I can write a book, I will get it published just like anyone else, and I just did.

Thank you for listening. Enjoy!

*THE PINK BUBBLE CHALLENGE*

1. Find me online, dancing to music
2. Get a library card and find a way to read
3. Find people to ask for help
4. Figure out your weaknesses and make a plan
5. Set up a profile for Meetup or local groups
6. If you need to change, do it
7. Join the pink bubble
8. Find ways to battle self talk issues
9. Research leadership techniques
10. Do the things you think you can't.

# This Doesn't Make Me An Expert

# MASTER BOOK LIST FOR LEARNING STUFF AND ALSO THINGS

### *Leadership*

- EntreLeadership: 20 Years of Practical Business Wisdom from the Trenches by Dave Ramsey A great book on being an entrepreneurial leader. This book gives you a practical, step by step guide on how to grow as a leader, how to develop the leaders around you and to get your business to where you want it to go.

- The Barefoot Executive: The Ultimate Guide for Being Your Own Boss and Achieving Financial Freedom by Carrie Wilkerson This is a great book to read before you embark on a life as a CEO of Me.

- Dare to Lead by Brene Brown: I love all of Brene's work but this is a great one for leaders to read. Also check out The Gifts of Imperfection and Rising Strongwhile you are at it.
- Developing the Leaders Around You: How to Help Others Reach Their Full Potential by John C. Maxwell I am a huge John C. Maxwell fan and would recommend pretty much all of his books. This book explains exactly what it's title eludes to.
- The 21 Irrefutable Laws of Leadership by John Maxwell Arguably, the best leadership book of all time. And, likely why it found its way to my top 10 recommended books.

*Productivity and Motivation*

- The 7 Habits of Highly Effective People:

Powerful Lessons in Personal Change (25th Anniversary Edition) by Stephen Covey. One of the best selling books ever, it is one that every small business owner needs to read to learn how to implement those 7 habits.

- The Secret by Rhonda Byrne. Hands down I can not stress how important The Law of Attraction is for life and for business.
- You Are A BadAss by Jen Sincero. THIS book changes everything. It is hilariously blunt but I loved every single word in this 27 chapter book about "How to Stop Doubting Your Greatness and Start Living an Awesome Life."
- The Art Of Happiness by the Dalai Lama. The tagline for this book is "A Handbook For Living." and that is so true. In this book the Dalai Lama answers life's most burning questions in a simple, optimistic, matter-of-fact

way.

- Awaken The Giant Within by Tony Robbins. An oldie but a goodie, Anthony Robbins is one of my all time favorite speakers, motivators and authors.
- Eat That Frog by Brian Tracy. The end-all book to conquering procrastination!! This book offers 21 methods for ending procrastination and getting more done each day.
- How to Win Friends and Influence People by Dale Carnegie If you haven't already read this classic, than you have some catching up to do.
- Outliers: The Story of Success –Malcolm Gladwell Success breeds success, so sales reps and young professionals looking to become successful should find models of similar success to emulate.

## Direct Sales Industry

- Be a Direct Selling Superstar: Achieve Financial Freedom for Yourself and Others as a Direct Sales Leader by Mary Christensen – A must read book for all direct sales and party plan reps from one of the top party plan reps. This is the book I read in the bath tub when I started.

- The Success Principles by Jack Canfield. Though this is a big, long book, I wanted to put it near the top because there is so much to learn just from this one single book

- Go Pro: 7 Steps to Becoming a Network Marketing Professional by Eric Worre In this guide-like format, this book will literally walk you through the top 7 actionable steps that anyone can apply to their business. Eric Worre is no stranger to this amazing profession and shares his 'aha' moments throughout.

- The Miracle Morning for Network Marketers: Grow yourself FIRST to Grow your Business Fast by Hal Elrod, Pat Petrini and Honoree Corder This recommended book is a great read for those who may have reached that plateau in their business.

*Business*

- Crush It by Gary Vaynerchuk How about taking your hobby, your obsession, your passion and all things in between and turning them into an income? This recommended read by Gary V., takes you on a journey of how to use the power of the internet to crush out your passion.
- The Infinite Game, by Simon Sinek A check-

ers match and the Super Bowl are finite games. Someone wins. Someone doesn't. Business, by contrast, is a ceaseless endeavor in which playing field, players, and rules change constantly.

- "Lean In: Women, Work, and the Will to Lead" by Sheryl Sandberg "Lean In" continues [the conversation around women in the workplace], combining personal anecdotes, hard data, and compelling research to change the conversation from what women can't do to what they can.

## Finances

- Rich Dad Poor Dad by Robert Kiyosaki. Another great book that teaches financial literacy to people in all walks of life!
- You Are a Badass at Making Money by Jen Sincero This book is candid and funny, and if

you're like many of us, you'll recognize yourself and your own habits in its pages. It's based on Sincero's personal experiences as she emerged from her salad days (although she preferred Taco Bell to cheap greens) to living very, very well.

*Sales*

- The Sales Bible: The Ultimate Sales Resource by Jeffrey Gitomer With another favorite sales book, Jeffrey Gitomer's The Sales Bible: The Ultimate Sales Resource, has been just that, the ultimate resource for thousands of sales professionals.
- How to Master the Art of Selling by Tom Hopkins With a new, revised edition, this book contains tips on how to become a better seller by utilizing email, various online resources,

and of course traditional sales methods.

- Coaching Salespeople into Sales Champions by Keith Rosen Want to learn the secret to building a successful sales team that will help you continuously increase your revenue? Keith Rosen sheds light on the ultimate tips and strategies to helping coach your sales reps to becoming high producers in a winning culture.
- Little Red Book of Selling: 12.5 Principles of Sales Greatness by Jeffrey Gitomer Are you on the impatient side and want better selling tips and answers given to you without having to read hundreds of pages? Then Jeffrey Gitomer has written the perfect book for you.
- Secrets of Closing the Sale by Zig Ziglar If you are a true sales person, than you must read Zig Ziglar's Secrets of Closing the Sale (or you

are ahead of the game and have already read it!).

- "The Psychology of Selling: Increase Your Sales Faster and Easier Than You Ever Thought Possible" Brian Tracy Learn how to harness psychological principles in the sales process while simultaneously getting a dose of personal motivation.

- "The Only Sales Guide You'll Ever Need" Anthony Iannarino Iannarino shares his biggest lessons from 25 years of selling, including how to increase your self-discipline, get over your fear of the competition, be more resourceful, discover the buyer's true needs, and more.

- "Words That Sell: More than 6000 Entries to Help You Promote Your Products, Services, and Ideas" Richard Bayan Keep this informative manual at your desk so you can quickly find the perfect terms and phrases to grab your prospect's attention, create desire for your product, and ultimately, win their business.

- "Go-Giver, Expanded Edition: A Little Story About a Powerful Business Idea" Bob Burg and John David Mann This quick read reveals the importance of giving to business success. Not only will you walk away convinced that giving leads to receiving, you'll also know how to give to achieve your desired results.

- "DISCOVER Questions Get You Connected" Deb Calvert and Renee Calvert Learn how to structure your calls, ask thoughtful, intelligent questions, and help prospects come to their own conclusions about your product's value.

- "Think and Grow Rich" Napoleon Hill This book is beloved by many career salespeople. The result of nearly 20 years of research, Hill's book outlines 13 steps to success, including developing a definite purpose, building a positive mental attitude, and channeling the power of the subconscious mind.

### Social media

- Trust Agents: Using the Web to Build Influence, Improve Reputation, and Earn Trust by Chris Brogan and Julien Smith This book is your guide to a new form of power broker–web natives who trade in trust, reputation, and relationships using tools you may never even have heard of.
- "Likeable Social Media" by Dave Kerpen Using clear how-to instructions, he provides

you with all of the information and tools necessary to engage customers in a digital world.

- "Jab, Jab, Jab, Right Hook" by Gary Vaynerchuk One of the easiest ways businesses can cut through the noise and deliver their message is through storytelling.

- "The Art of Social Media" by Guy Kawasaki & Peg Fitzpatrick Authors Guy Kawasaki and Peg Fitzpatrick team up to offer you a bottom-up strategy for creating a foundation, building your assets, attracting followers and integrating social media and blogging.

# EPILOGUE

The crazy thing that happens after I talk about all this stuff to people, they get this look on their face like a bus flew by. I want to be the first to tell you that this book is not meant to overwhelm but to be a resource to come back to over and over and over. Start somewhere, go one step at a time, take small bites. Do not attack this like you will be at the top of your game in a week. But also don't go so slow that you lose momentum. Step by step, you will build an empire that is not ignorable. I expect you to come find me with ink marks, scribbles, a highlighter, and dog ears. I do not want this book to be cherished but to be broken in and broken down. I want this to be info you read repeatedly and not just because you can't remember it all, but because you start to understand and crave the results around each turn. I only say that because when I started my first business I would do that to books. The info was so deep that I drank it all in while in the bath tub and spit it back out on to my team pages and the laps of great friends.

So if that is where you are at, be proud. You are about to dive into months or years of growth. I am over 5 years in and still returning to the basics that are in here. I'm always here if you need me, you can message me or chat on social. You are strong. You can do this. I do not need to know you to know that, you opened this book and read this far. You are already halfway to taking off like a comet so seatbelt in, let's not fear the first steps, and get to work!

See you on the social! I'll be watching with popcorn! <3

## ACKNOWLEDGEMENTS

To All My Amazing Parents. Life has not always been easy, but you have all tried your hardest to give me and our family every opportunity you could. As a parent, I have learned that is way more difficult than it looks as a teen. Thank you a million times.

To my husband and my babies, thank you for the patience and understanding while I hid in the basement and bathroom building a business and this book on borrowed time. I hope you always know it was for our future and can't wait to find new ways to make life amazing as we all grow up.

To my family for always offering a kind word

and reminding me that I can pull up my bootstraps and always keep going. You are some of the strongest people in my life facing deployments, illnesses, death, disorders, and divorce. I wouldn't have the strength inside of me without learning from all of you.

To my friends that helped me believe in myself and supported my many crazy ideas, you know who you are and you know I come up with REAL crazy ideas. Thanks for standing by me. Thank you for occasionally laughing at the bad ideas. Thanks for always threatening me with a martini and a good time. We have been through so much, I am glad we have each other.

To Jess Mastorakos, thank you for answering all my messages on how to self publish. You have some amazing knowledge. Special shouts to the Beta Readers and Volunteer editing from friends and family, you helped me put it all into words. Thank you for translating all this passion. If you were one of the first 300 to read the first chapter, this is your shout also! You guys seriously give me life.

To my teammates that believed in a bright pink dream, thank you for trusting me as I have learned and grown. To my sponsor Lauren Rush, I can never repay you for the blessings you have brought into my life. You are forever in my heart and in my life, so you are stuck with me. To our leader Shaleen Ague, I can not imagine the patience it takes to answer all my questions.

To the corporate office for the direct sales

company I joined and l have earned so much from, it has been amazing getting to watch you grow in the last 7 years and I am so excited about all the possibilities and opportunities ahead. We are so blessed with people that always believe in our businesses. Thank you for the late nights, the ugly mornings, the long support requests, and the critical thinking. It is seen.

Made in the USA
Lexington, KY
29 January 2019